PASTORS, PARISHES AND PEOPLE IN SURREY

David Robinson

GW00505058

Published by

PHILLIMORE

for

SURREY LOCAL HISTORY COUNCIL

1989

1989
Published by
PHILLIMORE & CO. LTD.
Shopwyke Hall,
Chichester, Sussex, England

for
SURREY LOCAL HISTORY COUNCIL
Guildford, Surrey

as extra volume number one of
Surrey History

ISBN 0 85033 708 9

Cover Illustration Plate I: ADORATION OF THE SHEPHERDS: a brass of c.1500, once part of a larger memorial brass in Cobham Church. Jesus in the manger is in the centre. The Virgin Mary lies on a low wooden bed in the foreground, with her head on a cushion. Joseph is to the left and the shepherds are on the right.

FOREWORD

IN 1984 THE SURREY LOCAL HISTORY COUNCIL selected 'Surrey Churches' as the subject of their annual symposium. They invited me to give an outline of the history of the church in Surrey and I attempted to take my audience from the seventh century to the beginning of the twentieth in the course of a single hour. My aim was to give local historians an impression of the spirit of Christian life and organisation in each period, using Surrey examples as illustrations. I omitted descriptions of church architecture, which was excellently covered by another speaker, Mr. Mervyn Blatch. My talk was given on the basis of such published and archival evidence as lay readily to hand, supplemented by brief visits to the Winchester diocesan records at the Hampshire Record Office and the Surrey archdeaconry records at the Greater London Record Office.

A number of members of my audience suggested that the talk should be published. In preparing the manuscript for publication I have attempted to fill gaps and tie up loose ends, without destroying the outline character of the work. There remains a certain imbalance in my treatment of different periods, subjects and parts of the county, reflecting the deficiences of my own knowledge and the material available to me. In two respects this booklet provides an old-fashioned kind of local history. I have not carried out detailed research to quantify the evidence and establish how typical my examples are, nor have I been able to isolate a specifically Surrey religious ethos which might be contrasted with that of other counties or to compare different areas within the county. Nevertheless I hope that this booklet may help those who study the history of an individual church to set their findings in a broader context and that it may interest all who are concerned for the history of the churches in Surrey. In general, I have restricted myself to Surrey outside 'inner London'. Southwark, Lambeth and Wandsworth would require separate study, especially for the nineteenth century, and it seemed better not to let them over-balance the booklet. I have also not attempted to cover Spelthorne, which has only formed part of Surrey since 1965.

I must express my thanks to my colleagues in the Surrey Record Office at County Hall, Kingston-upon-Thames, and the Guildford Muniment Room for their kind assistance, and indeed their labours over many years to preserve, list and make available the records on which research of this kind relies, and to my fellow archivists at the Hampshire Record Office, especially Miss White, and at the Greater London Record Office, especially Mrs. Keneally, for service well beyond the call of normal professional duty. A work of this kind depends on the ready availability of source-material for research and I and countless other historians owe a great debt to the clergy and congregations of the churches for their responsible action in placing their records in record offices for safe keeping and public access, and to the governing bodies of the various churches for encouraging such action. The Surrey County Library Service, and in particular Lesley Pratt of the County Hall Reference Centre, were indefatigable in obtaining published works for me. I am especially grateful to Kenneth Gravett, Chairman of the Surrey Local History Council, for advice on the text and assistance with illustrations.

I would like to dedicate this booklet to Isobel, churchwarden, archivist, wife and mother, in whose absence at church council and committee meetings so much of it has been written.

David Robinson

Kingston-upon-Thames.
August 1988.

PLATES

PASTORS, PARISHES AND PEOPLE IN SURREY

THE CONTINUOUS STORY OF CHRISTIANITY IN SURREY, as in most parts of England, begins with the conversion of the English between the sixth and the eighth centuries. Although Christ was worshipped in Roman Britain - Constantine, born in Britain, established Christianity as the official religion of the Empire - the Angles, Saxons and Jutes who invaded in the fifth and sixth centuries brought with them the worship of Germanic gods such as Thunor, the god of thunder, and the warrior gods, Tiwe and Woden. Evidence that the Saxons who settled in Surrey retained their beliefs for a considerable period is found in places named after their gods, such as Thursley and Tuesley, groves sacred to Thunor and Tiwe, and Thunderfield, Thunor's open land.

The existing inhabitants, of Celtic and Roman stock - 'Welsh' as the invaders called them - were subjugated, except in Wales and for a time Cornwall. The Surrey place-names Walton-on-Thames and Wallington, the hamlets of the Welsh, suggest that they were not wiped out but that they predominated in only a few locations. Some Christian centres may have survived from Roman times: in Surrey it has been tentatively suggested that the name of an enclosure or meadow called in a tenth-century charter 'eccles hamme' - 'eccles' (from the latin *ecclesia*) a church and 'hamme' a meadow or enclosure - near the site later chosen for Bisley church may imply contact between the Germanic settlers and a Romano-Celtic Christian cult centred on a church site or the holy well of St. John the Baptist. Despite this the historian Bede's condemnation of the Britons for not preaching the Christian faith to the Saxon and Angle settlers seems to be justified.

The conversion of Southern England followed the landing of Augustine in Kent in 597. The Saxons of Surrey were presumably converted in the seventh century: the first recorded Christian enterprise in the county was the foundation of Chertsey 'minster' in 666. Chertsey seems to have been the earliest minster in Surrey. Minsters were churches of a public character - not private chapels - founded by kings, or by bishops under royal patronage, in important administrative centres. Chertsey may have initially served the territory of the Woccingas who gave their name to Woking, although a separate minster was founded at Woking within a few decades. There is only scanty evidence of the foundation and early history of most of the Surrey minsters. Farnham, Godalming, Kingston-upon-Thames and probably Southwark, Leatherhead, Godstone, Croydon and Stoke-by-Guildford seem to have completed a network of perhaps ten minsters by the ninth century. The Christian missionaries may have deliberately taken existing religious sites and converted them to Christian use: Farnham was in the centre of a heathen religious complex with Peper Harow ('Pippra's temple') and Thursley not far away. The site of the original Godalming minster seems to have been at Tuesley and Godstone was not far from Thunderfield. The minster was the ecclesiastical centre of a *parochia* which might comprise the areas of between five and fifteen later parishes and probably coincided with an administrative and economic unit which was the larger predecessor of the medieval 'hundred'. The minster was staffed by a community

1

of clergy who might be monks but were more often 'secular' (non-monastic) clergy called canons, who lived a corporate life together without taking monastic vows. We do not know whether the canons served their parishioners primarily by visiting outlying settlements or whether the parishioners normally came to the mother-church, but by the end of the tenth century no part of the county outside the still-uncolonised Wealden forest in the south was more than about six miles from a minster. The minster clergy were supported by endowments of land and by the 'tithe' (tenth) of the produce of their parishioners.

The relationship between the minster and the pattern of secular lordship reflected in miniature the relationship between the kingdom of Wessex, with its capital at Winchester, and the cathedral church of Wessex, located at Winchester. Surrey, as part of Wessex, became part of the diocese of Winchester. Other dioceses were later founded in western Wessex but the diocese of Winchester continued to cover Hampshire and Surrey.

What turned the Germanic settlers to Christianity ? Perhaps it was in part a continuing reverence for the name and reputation of Rome and in part an awareness of the cultural heritage of Christian France and Italy, but there was also the attraction of Christianity as an articulated and satisfying system of belief. A story told by Bede in his account of the conversion of Northumbria shows its appeal. One of King Edwin's councillors compared the life of man to a sparrow flying through the king's hall in winter. Inside the hall there is a fire and the storm does not touch it, but when the sparrow passes outside it disappears from sight. 'If the new teaching brings more knowledge of what lies beyond the present life', he said, 'let them follow it'. The success of Christianity was dependent on a warrior aristocracy and the English took over as the object of their worship a Christ who, even in His sufferings, possessed the attributes of a hero. In the Old English poem, *The Dream of the Rood*, the Cross itself speaks:

"Then I saw mankind's Lord Hasten with great valour to climb on me . . . . .
The young hero stripped himself That was God Almighty
Strong and resolute Mounted He the gallows
Brave in men's sight He would ransom mankind".

Parishes and Parish Churches

The Danish invasions of the ninth century probably broke the continuity of minster life - Chertsey minster was destroyed by the Danes - and the authority of the minster churches was permanently impaired by a new institution, the estate church. Between the ninth and eleventh centuries the larger jurisdictional and economic communities which the minsters served began to break up into independent manors and villages. The people who settled these villages wanted their own local churches. Their lords provided these churches and appointed priests to serve them, for their tenants' benefit and to secure the permanent endowment of masses and prayers for their own souls. The churches founded on the royal manors of Reigate, Dorking and Shere and on the manors of Shalford, Witley and Oxted, which belonged to 'thegns' (local lords), are examples of pre-Domesday, and probably pre-Norman, foundations.

For a time, minsters and local estate churches co-existed, but the minsters were under attack. The reforming bishops of the tenth century - Archbishop Dunstan,

2

Oswald of Worcester and, especially, Aethelwold of Winchester - saw them as corrupt institutions staffed by clergy who did not observe the Benedictine monastic rule and who had in some cases carved private estates out of the original endowments of the minster. In 964 King Edgar, probably at Aethelwold's insistence, expelled the canons of Chertsey and replaced them by monks.

Corrupt or not, the minsters were losing their purpose as the village churches took over their pastoral duties. Most minsters became ordinary parish churches. One or two, such as Kingston and Farnham, prevented other local churches from becoming more than chapels and their own parishes remained large, covering almost all of the original *parochia*. The parish of Kingston extended from Kew to East Molesey and included chapels at Shene (Richmond), Petersham, Thames Ditton and East Molesey. Farnham parish included Frensham, Seale and Elstead, with Bentley in Hampshire. Each of these parishes roughly coincided with the local government area, the 'hundred', of the same name. Godalming minster, on the other hand, originally no doubt covering the whole hundred of Godalming as far as the Sussex and Hampshire boundaries, was reduced to normal parochial size as parishes were carved out of it.

By the time of Domesday Book there were about sixty to seventy churches which would become parochial in the course of the middle ages, more than half of the eventual number of medieval parish churches. These stood mainly on manors of the Crown, the Archbishops of Canterbury and a few leading nobles, and on the outlying manors of the estates belonging to religious houses. Chertsey Abbey, for example, had founded churches on its more distant estates, such as Great Bookham, Coulsdon, Epsom and Sutton, by 1086, but only later 'infilled' with churches at Egham, Thorpe, Cobham and Weybridge, which were nearer to the mother house. The infeudation of manors by large landowners to smaller ones produced further church foundations, especially on the Downs, and others came as the Weald was colonised. Along the dip-slope of the Downs, Ilbert de Lacy or his successor Hugh Laval built Cuddington in about 1100, Lawrence de Rouen built Ashtead a little later, and Little Bookham, Fetcham and Effingham were built before the mid-twelfth century. Hambledon, Leigh, Horne, Burstow and Crowhurst may all be examples of the foundation of churches in the Weald as the 'denns' - pasture attached to distant estates - became distinct economic and tenurial entities.

The emergence of estate churches complicated the ecclesiastical pattern. They could be, in effect, islands in an area dependent on a minster, with local tenants still owing some dues to the minster as mother-church. The bishops tried to create from this complicated network of overlapping rights a regular parochial structure. They favoured the claims of estate churches to independent status as parish churches. The areas of the parishes expanded to meet each other and their boundaries were delineated. Their rights were standardised: the marks of an independent parish were usually that its church had the burial ground in which the parishioners were buried and that its priests had security of tenure and the right to receive tithes.

By about 1300, there was little doubt which churches were full parish churches and which were only chapels. One chapel, Ewkenes, in the south of the large parish of Dorking, managed to become an independent parish as late as the fourteenth century: it retains today the name 'Capel' (*capella*, chapel). Thorpe in the parish of Egham was granted parochial status by Bishop Beaufort as late as 1428. These were exceptions. Haslemere, founded in the thirteenth century by the

Bishop of Salisbury as a 'new town', could not escape from subservience to its mother church and remained a chapel of Chiddingfold until 1869.

The shape of the parish reflected the patterns of agriculture and land ownership. The parishes of southern Surrey, such as Tandridge, Godstone, Abinger and Wotton, extended over chalk, greensand and Wealden clay, which gave each one a balanced economy. The parishes from West Clandon to Croydon on the dip slope of the chalk had similarly long, narrow shapes. Parishes might not form single geographical entities. Many of them, especially in the south of the county, such as Charlwood, Tandridge, Dunsfold, Hascombe, Ewhurst and Cranleigh, included detached portions, which might represent outliers of the agricultural economy - clearings in woodland used as pasture, for example - or outlying parts of the manor of the lord who founded the parish.

The county of Surrey remained part of the diocese of Winchester until the nineteenth century. It formed a single archdeaconry - the archdeaconry of Surrey - and was divided into three rural deaneries: Ewell, Guildford (later Stoke) and Southwark. The Archbishops of Canterbury, who owned extensive estates in the county, on which they had founded churches, were able to exclude the bishop's and archdeacon's authority and to exercise their own 'peculiar' jurisdiction over their parishes: Croydon, East Horsley, Merstham, Wimbledon, Barnes, Burstow, Newington, Cheam and Charlwood.

The Medieval Clergyman

The bishops were determined to make the clergy constitutionally independent of their secular lords and the right of the founder of a parish church and his successors to install their own man as priest and to dismiss him at will was whittled down to the right, as 'patron', to 'present' or nominate a candidate to the bishop, who, if the man were suitable, would institute him to the church. The bishop could reject a man only if he were legally unqualified - too young, illiterate or of manifestly bad character. He could not resist him on the grounds of general unsuitability but there was at least a curb on the lord's right to appoint a totally unfit person. The priest, once instituted and installed in his benefice, could not be deprived of it except by due process of law for a proven offence: such deprivations were very rare. He had a life freehold in his office and its endowments and was independent of the displeasure both of his lord and his bishop.

What were the endowments of the benefice? There was the glebe, land which was given by the lord and which the priest himself could cultivate or could let to a farmer. The glebe was often similar in acreage to a sizeable peasant holding: thirty acres at Ashtead, twenty-five at Beddington, twenty-two at Farleigh. A few churches had much larger glebes, including the well-endowed former minsters of Godalming and Leatherhead and those churches such as Ockley (95 acres) in the Weald and Chobham (72 acres) and Worplesdon (62 acres) in north-western Surrey which may have benefited from late colonisation of wood or heath.

The tithes were the other main endowment. The priest received one-tenth of the corn harvest and of wool and lambs - the 'great tithes'. He also received one tenth of other produce - the 'small tithes' - and, so far as he could collect them, tithes or payment *in lieu* from craftsmen, traders and others whose income derived from less easily taxable sources. The third source of income consisted of various minor payments, including Easter payments and altar dues. The whole

4

II CHALDON CHURCH WALL PAINTING, c.1200: Small figures scramble up the central ladder towards heaven, the arc at the top. The upper half of the picture shows, on the left, the weighing of souls by the Archangel Michael and, on the right, Christ 'harrowing Hell', after his Crucifixion and before his Resurrection. The lower half shows Hell, with a cauldron on the left and two devils holding a saw on the right. On the far right is the tree of knowledge of good and evil.

III MAP OF PARISHES IN SOUTHERN SURREY: This map, based on mid-nineteenth-century Ordnance Survey maps, shows the complex parochial geography which derived from medieval patterns of land settlement and ownership.

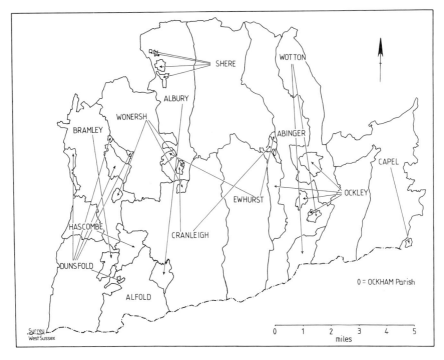

IV OAKWOOD CHAPEL: A simple thirteenth-century chapel in the Weald, south-west of Ockley but on the borders of Abinger parish and a detached part of Wotton.

V JOHN SWETECOK: Memorial brass to John Swetecok, master of Lingfield College, d.1459, in Lingfield church.

income might add up to a nominal value of £10 to £20 by the late thirteenth century, although this almost certainly underestimates the true value of the parish to a resident rector: it may approximately represent the sum for which a non-resident could let the income of his benefice.

Many laymen, however, passed over to religious houses the patronage of the churches they had founded. The monks or nuns might well consider that they needed part of the income of the benefice for their own maintenance. In such cases the monastery normally got two-thirds of the income, and became in effect the rector - the term used was usually 'impropriator'- and appointed a vicar (*vicarius* means deputy) who received the other third. Vicars were generally poorer than rectors, although a few vicarages, such as those of Farnham and Godalming, were in such rich parishes that even on one-third of the income the vicar was better off than many rectors. Vicars were also obliged, at least until the later middle ages, to reside in their parishes and to serve them in person. This, as well as their lower value, made vicarages unattractive to an important class of clergy, those who used their benefices as financial support while they were employed in non-parochial work.

For who were the beneficed clergy? Until late in the middle ages they comprised almost the whole body of literate men. The king needed his 'king's clerks' to be his judges and administrators. Bishops needed clerks to run their dioceses. Universities needed them for teaching. The local knights needed them to act as their scribes and write their title deeds. There was little money directly available to pay for regular service: kings paid for their own judiciary and civil service from the income of their own estates and bishops used their estates to support their diocesan officers and the judges of their ecclesiastical courts. They, together with monasteries and knights, therefore, often provided for these servants by appointing them to benefices in their patronage. Kings and knights provided for their relations in the same way. They had endowed the churches richly and would reap a return from them.

The Crown set an example by the exercise of its own influence over the appointment of bishops. Winchester was the richest diocese in the country and its early medieval bishops were men of high birth and ability, who filled the great offices of state. Henry of Blois (1129-71), 'monk and warrior', was brother of King Stephen and, as papal legate, was for a time probably the most powerful man in England. Peter des Roches (1205-38) was punningly described by a contemporary as 'hard as a rock' and governed the country as justiciar in 1213 in the absence of King John. Several of the later medieval bishops, such as William Edenton (1346-66) and William of Wykeham (1367-1404), were of humbler birth but by their ability had become leading administrators. Their appointments were reflected at parochial level. Rectors of Wimbledon included several clerks of the king or queen, most notably Walter Reynolds, rector 1295-1310, who became Archbishop of Canterbury, and his successor, John de Sandale, rector 1310-16, Chancellor of the Exchequer, Lord Chancellor and later Bishop of Winchester. Such appointments, although made for secular purposes, were not necessarily harmful to the church. The medieval Bishops of Winchester administered their diocese efficiently, were liberal benefactors of their cathedral church and founded religious, charitable and educational establishments. Within the parish, a good deputy under the occasional supervision of a really able man might be better than a run-of-the-mill clergyman with no effective superior.

The rector or vicar was not the only clergyman in the parish. There would also be a parish chaplain or parish priest to assist a resident incumbent or replace an absent one. In addition there might be other priests employed to say masses for the living and the dead. These included chantry chaplains with permanent endowments, priests employed by guilds or fraternities (benevolent and convivial societies), priests employed to say masses for a man's or woman's soul for a year or two after their death, and priests - in effect 'jobbing priests' - who would say masses as and when anyone would pay for them. Chantries were to be found in many churches. At Croydon there were the chantry of Our Lady and the chantry of St. Nicholas; at Bagshot chapel there was Hughlettes chantry, the priest of which might perform the regular worship of the chapel in the absence of any other priest. At Dorking a fraternity paid for a priest to pray for the souls of its brothers and sisters. At Witley a rent of 6s. a year paid for a priest to say mass at harvest time. In 1501 Robert Somerby, Vicar of Kingston, left money in his will for monthly celebrations in the parish church during the year after his death: this would give temporary employment to the clerical equivalent of the casual labourer. Grandest of the Surrey chantries was Lingfield College, founded in 1431 by Sir Reginald Cobham and endowed with the rectorial income. The provost, five chaplains, four clerks and thirteen paupers were employed primarily to pray for the souls of the deceased, although the collegiate clergy were also responsible for the parochial duty. Here the chantry swallowed up the parish church.

The Bishops of Winchester had no illusions about the standard of their clergy and thirteenth-century bishops tried to control their behaviour by statutes. Clergy were, according to Bishop Peter des Roches in 1225, not to defame their order by their tonsure, habit or gait; in singing and ministering in church they were to behave properly, neither laughing nor chatting, and if it were necessary to say anything to any one, they were to do so with lowered voice and few words. Clergy with the cure of souls were to live honestly and serve their ministry faithfully; they were not to omit saying the canonical hours and were to say these distinctly and with devotion, not hurrying or slurring the words. Beneficed clergy were to be hospitable and not niggardly towards the poor - 'as it is written "What the clergy have is the poor's" '. Parish priests were to preach the Word of God regularly to their people and must go quickly and gladly to the sick when they were summoned. Under Bishop Raleigh's statutes of c.1247, clergy were not to attend plays and entertainments by minstrels and jugglers and, 'because the humility of Jesus Christ and evangelical perfection demand that if anyone is struck on one cheek he is to turn the other one', they were not to carry arms. Bishop Gervais in the 1260s ordered archdeacons to enquire carefully whether rectors and vicars were deficient in letters and whether parish priests had at least a simple understanding of the faith and knew the Ten Commandments, the seven sacraments and seven deadly sins and could expound these in the vulgar tongue to the people in their charge.

Church Buildings and Ornaments

The size and condition of the church itself depended on the wealth and devotion of the clergy and people. The rector was usually responsible for the upkeep of the chancel: the people maintained the nave. In the absence of outside assistance for church building, the size and sophistication of the nave, in particular, reflected local wealth or poverty and the date of the surviving fabric might be an indication of the period of greatest wealth. Surrey was not a rich county and it does not possess the great village churches of wealthier areas; the Early English and Decorated churches of the agrarian east midlands or the Perpendicular 'woollen' churches of the west country. Town churches, such as Farnham, Kingston and Reigate, were quite large. Most village churches were small by the standards of richer counties and the churches of hamlets such as Farleigh, Wisley and Pyrford were very small.

Inside the church there was a font for baptising each child and bringing it into the ambit of salvation - the church as a body as well as the church as a building. At the chancel arch was a screen - the rood screen - bearing the figure of the crucified Christ between his Mother and St. John. At the east end was the high altar at which the main mass was celebrated, but the church might contain several altars at which other clergy said their masses. There might be stained-glass images of saints in the windows: SS. Peter and Paul at Buckland, for example, and the Virgin and Child at Compton. The walls would be painted and the Purgatorial Ladder which still remains at Chaldon, with its picture of heaven, hell and purgatory, is a vivid reminder that the medieval church was as committed as any seventeenth-century Puritan divine or stern Victorian parent to the saving of souls by fear if need be. There might be pews - Dunsfold has some of the earliest and best surviving - but most of the nave was open and the congregation stood or knelt.

The Sunday high mass was the centre of worship. The incumbent, supported by assistant priests and chantry chaplains, chanted it at the high altar, while the people recited their prayers in the nave. The service might be a richly beautiful one in a town church with many assistant priests and a rich range of vestments. Elsewhere it was no doubt less impressive but the stone building lit by oil lamps and candles, with the clergy decked in robes of some richness, gave villagers a vision of a world beyond their own temporary hovels.

The church, in its attempt to explain the faith to an illiterate congregation, and perhaps for more self-indulgent reasons, was a cradle of English drama. In Kingston the Resurrection was re-enacted with a dramatic bang! In 1519 the churchwardens spent 8d. on 'a skynne of parchement and for Gunpowder for the play on Easter Day' and 14d. for bread and ale for 'them that made the stage at Easter and other things that belongyth to the play'.

Churches needed for their worship a variety of ornaments and vestments. The size and wealth of parishes was reflected in these as in the church buildings. By the mid-sixteenth century, Oxted, a small country parish, possessed two silver chalices, copes of silk, cloth of gold and green velvet, three or four silk vestments and vestments of red velvet and satin, two silk and two white satin tunicles, three velvet corporal covers and a corporal cloth, a red velvet hearse cloth, three streamers and a veil, and it had four bells in the steeple, sanctus bells and two processional bells. Holy Trinity, Guildford, a town church, was provided with more and costlier items, perhaps some sixty or seventy in all, and including four great candlesticks, a full set of vestments of cloth of gold for priest, deacon and subdeacon, a cope of blue velvet bordered with flowers and one of blue 'baudekin' (a rich cloth) with peacocks, a red silk canopy, nine surplices 'good and bad', two organs and a portative organ, - organs were common in town churches by the sixteenth century - 'two littell towels for to wype the prestes hands' and 'a littell blew vestyment for every daye'. At the other extreme, the tiny parish of Gatton, already almost depopulated by the early sixteenth century, possessed only a cope and vestment of old blue satin, 'a vestment of rotten dornix' (Tournai cloth), ' a bell not lowde inowghe to be hard a flight shotte agaynst the wynde', a rusty holy water 'stocke' (stoup) with two cruets and a corporal, two ragged linen altar cloths and a pair of altar cloths of old 'saye' (a fine-textured cloth) and a chalice borrowed from Chipstead church 'for that whyche dyd aperteyne to the church was broken'.

The goods presented by the parishioners were the responsibility of officers elected by the parishioners. Churchwardens took responsibility for the fabric of the church, and in particular the nave and tower. Their assets included gifts and bequests of objects and money. They could levy a rate to raise income. Other officers might also be appointed - when Margaret, widow of William Smith, granted land to endow an oil lamp in Witley church and one in Thursley church for the souls of her late husband and herself, their parents and benefactors and all the faithful departed, the lamps were committed to the care of the *'custodes luminarium'* (lamp wardens) of the churches.

Belief and Practice

This was the structure of the medieval parish. What was the faith which held it together? Until recently, local historians tended to commit themselves to one of two conflicting assessments of medieval Christianity. Protestant writers believed that a bigoted and superstitious clergy had kept the people in ignorance and fear until the dawning of the Reformation. Roman Catholics and Anglo-Catholics regarded medieval life as a happy round of religious and secular celebrations, centred around the church in worship and festivals - the conjunction of 'holy day' and 'holiday' - until the Reformation cast its chill blight on both sacred and secular pleasures.

Medieval bishops did not see life in these clear-cut ways. Like later Puritan preachers they regarded the general mass of men and women as sinful and needing to be controlled by a stern, although in intention fatherly, discipline. When the thirteenth-century Bishops of Winchester issued their statutes, they showed their awareness that the laity had retained or acquired a sense of the supernatural which did not necessarily run in orthodox Christian channels: priests could declare excommunication on those practising sorcery, and no stones, wood, trees or wells were to be venerated as holy on account of dreams 'for in these ways we believe that many dangers threaten the souls of the faithful'. The bishops used their authority in secular matters also. They forbade mothers lying with, and risking overlying, their children in bed, and condemned the exposure of children. Evidence of the behaviour of laymen and women is found in a visitation book of about 1515. Alice Ambrose and Joan Chapman of Ewell were common scolds. Margery Roke, a suspect woman, was not to visit Chertsey Abbey. Richard Whitfield of Ewell did not know how many mortal sins there were: he was told that there were seven. He was then asked how many Commandments there were and hopefully answered 'seven'. He was also told that there were seven corporal acts of mercy and was told to learn them and pay ½d. for each of the acts of mercy. The usual punishment for moral offences was likely to be a penance, perhaps, as with a Kingston fornicator, to go round the market place dressed only in his shirt and on Sunday to go similarly in procession with a wax candle in his hand to the high altar, to kneel there until the offertory at high mass, and then to offer the candle to the hands of the priest celebrating.

By this time, however, the diocesan authorities were fighting a more serious threat than immorality. In the second half of the fourteenth century John Wycliffe had promoted doctrines which would later be shared by the Protestant reformers and for the next 150 years groups of followers of his teachings - Lollards - came to the surface from time to time. They studied the Bible for themselves, doubted the Real Presence of Christ in the Eucharist, attacked the veneration of images and criticised the authority of the priesthood. In 1440 John Witton, Rector of Chiddingfold, was charged with heresy regarding the Eucharist, pilgrimages and the veneration of images. He denied the charges, but admitted that he feared that simple people were deluded into worshipping images. In the same year a group of Lollards in the area around Odiham and Crondall in Hampshire and Farnham in Surrey, including a Farnham weaver and a former chaplain of Thursley, were charged with heresy and sedition.

In 1513 a group of Kingston heretics were tried in Southwark priory. One of them, Thomas Denys of Malden, had already been found guilty of heresy twenty years earlier at Waltham in Essex. Now he was accused of asserting that 'the sacrement of the altar in fourme of brede was not the veray body of Criste but a commemoration of Cristes passion and Christes body in a figure and not the veray body' and that 'oblations to images in the church' were 'but idolatrie and nothing worth for they were but stokkes and stones made by manys handes'. He had denied the special power of priests to forgive sins; any man could 'assoile and make forgiveness'. The diocesan officers declared that 'it is not lawful for thee or any other and most specially not lay persons for to make doubts reason or dispute openly or privily of the faith of Criste and of the determinations of our Moder Holy Church or of the absolute power of our holy father the pope or for to move or hold any erroneous opinions disputations or questions against the determinations of holy church'. Denys confessed his offence and was absolved from his excommunication and received back into the bosom and unity of the holy mother church, but the infection of heresy, which could lead to the damnation of others, must be stamped out, and he was handed over to the secular authorities and burnt to death in Kingston market place.

The medieval church was proving inadequate with the new spread of learning but while it retained political power it was safe. Once it lost that power it was unable to retain its hold on men's hearts and minds, except in a few families in the south east of England and rather more widely in some of the remoter counties.

The Reformation in Surrey

In the 1530s Henry VIII broke with Rome and renounced papal jurisdiction over England. Soon afterwards he dissolved the monasteries. English-language Bibles were placed in the churches, but in general Henry and the English church retained the distinctive Catholic beliefs and practices: the Latin mass with rich ornaments, a celibate priesthood, prayers for the dead.

Reformed doctrine and worship became predominant only after Henry's death in 1547. During the reign of his son Edward VI collegiate churches and chantries were abolished - a few such as Lingfield had already gone - clergy were allowed to marry and the rich furnishings were removed from parish churches. The Church adopted first of all an English Communion service, then in 1549 an English, but still fairly Catholic, Prayer Book, and finally in 1552 a distinctively Protestant Prayer Book. After Edward's death in 1553 his sister, Queen Mary, restored papal authority and Catholic practices, although she was unable to prise out of laymen the monastic estates they had acquired. During the later part of her reign there was a determined effort to extirpate reformed belief and men and women were executed as heretics.

What did people make of the changes? Henry VIII's actions provoked little reaction in the country. Kings of England had already severely restricted the practical scope of papal authority and unimpeachably Catholic monarchs such as the Kings of Spain and France had established control over the churches in their territories. A few men, notably Sir Thomas More and John Fisher, Bishop of Rochester, were executed for their allegiance to the pope and the universal church, but most bishops, priests and laity saw little to challenge their consciences. Stephen Gardiner became Bishop of Winchester in 1531 and was a stalwart supporter of royal supremacy while resisting changes in sacramental doctrine.

Attitudes hardened during the switchback changes of the next dozen years. Bishop Gardiner was unable to accept Edward's doctrinal changes and was imprisoned in 1548. In 1551, he was deprived of his see and replaced by John Ponet, Bishop of Rochester, a committed reformer. Ponet in turn was replaced by Gardiner on Mary's accession and went into exile, dying at Strasbourg in 1556. Gardiner himself died in 1555. He was succeeded by John White, who had emerged even in Edward's reign as an opponent of reformed practices.

Nevertheless Surrey seems to have been a fairly conformist county. Few Surrey clergymen took advantage of the opportunity of marrying during Edward VI's reign, unlike, for example, those of strongly Protestant Essex. The county was little touched by Mary's persecution. Wills provide evidence of Surrey's conformity. In Henry VIII's reign most testators prefaced their wills with traditional Catholic formulae commending their souls to the protection of the Blessed Virgin Mary and the saints. Under Edward VI most wills are prefaced either by specifically Protestant formulae, in which the testator declares his trust solely in the merits of Jesus Christ, or by non-specific commendations. Catholic formulae again predominate in the first half of Mary's reign, although after 1556, contrary to the overall pattern of conformity, they are in the minority, many testators using imprecise phrases. Most testators from early in Elizabeth's reign again used positively Protestant formulations.

The laity took what they could of church lands and church goods. The parochial tithes which the monasteries had appropriated were taken over by laymen and were not restored to the vicars; from the dissolution of the monasteries onwards the greater part of the tithes in many parishes was paid to laymen, called lay impropriators or lay rectors. In Lingfield, when the collegiate church was dissolved in 1544, there was left to serve the parish only a chaplain paid a small and uncertain stipend.

The churchwardens acted swiftly once they knew that the rich ornaments of medieval worship were to be disposed of. By realising their assets they could pay for repairs to the church and for work necessitated by Protestant innovations. The churchwardens of Betchworth sold alabaster tables to John Frenchman of Horsham for 3s., gold images to the parson of St. Edmunds, Lombard Street, for

VI WILLIAM OUGHTRED, 1575-1660: Oughtred, the leading mathematician of his day was successively rector of Guildford St. Mary, Shalford and Albury.

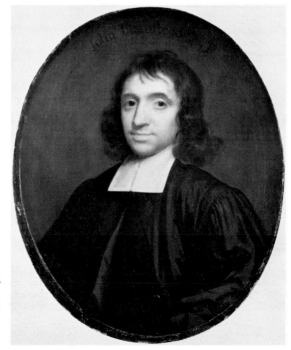

VII JOHN FLAMSTEED, 1646-1719: Flamsteed, rector of Burstow from 1684 to his death, was the first Astronomer Royal. His 'British Catalogue' of stars was the first collection of its kind, made with telescope and clock.

VIII LONG DITTON CHURCH: This is Sir Robert Taylor's design of 1776. The tower and cupola were never built and the church was replaced, after some controversy, by a gothic revival church by G.E. Street in 1878-80.

5s. and part of the tabernacle for 7s. An altar stone was bought by one of the wardens himself for 3s. This, with other money, was spent on repairing a buttress, mending the church pavement and gutters and windows, white-liming and rough-casting the church and steeple, making five seats, a ladder and a bell wheel and three bell ropes, pulling down the altars and carrying the stones out of the church and acquiring the Book of Common Prayer, a psalter and a Book of Homilies.

These changes were reversed during Mary's reign: at Wandsworth in 1553-4 the churchwardens paid 4d. for carriage of stone to make up an altar, 5s. for a new missal and £3 10s. 10d. for a chalice, and in 1556-7 they paid £5 for 'the making of the Rood with Mary and John'. After the accession of Elizabeth, Catholic furnishings were again removed and were nowhere restored before the nineteenth century. The Kingston churchwardens in 1560-1 bought four bushels of lime 'to make [good] the place where the altar stoode' and received 11s. for an old cope and 40s. for a cope, a vestment and three banner cloths. In 1563, 25s. 5d. was paid for 'newe glassynge of the west wyndowe', in 1566, 46 feet of new glass were provided for the Lady window and in 1569, 9d. was received for 'owld peeces of glasse that were in the store howse': presumably these payments mark the replacement of painted glass by clear glass.

Such changes may have induced in many incumbents and churchwardens an attitude of wariness towards expenditure on church fabrics. In 1569-70, 24 Surrey churches had chancels described as 'ruinosus' and ten 'churches' (probably meaning the naves) were described in the same way, although 'ruinosus' does not necessarily imply that the church was literally in ruins.

Elizabeth sought to encompass as many of the people as possible in her settle-ment of religion. Nevertheless, none of the Marian bishops conformed - Bishop White of Winchester, like the others, was deprived of his see - and a number of Surrey clergy were deprived of their benefices in the early 1560s. For the first ten years the government was tolerant of Catholic dissent but, following the pope's excommunication of Elizabeth in 1570, the government began to crack down on Roman Catholics. Surrey was not affected by strong Roman Catholic recusancy although a number of families, such as the Copleys of Gatton and Leigh, were recusant. Nevertheless, after the Spanish Armada in 1588 a number of priests and laymen were executed, the first being William Way at or near Kingston on 23rd. September 1588.

Clergy of the Reformation Period

The establishment of Reformed worship presented problems for the successful party. The Catholic priest had needed to read the services and care for his flock. He had also needed to give them simple teaching, but he had been able to appeal to the authority of the church in his teaching and had not needed to expound scripture and doctrine at length, arguing maybe with a more articulate laity which had been made to question by the changes in doctrine and worship of recent years. Crown, bishops, Puritan divines and laymen and women, by endowing colleges, provided increased opportunities for potential clergymen to study at university. In the 1520s about one third of the clergy beneficed in Surrey were graduates. A century later nearly all of them were graduates and the non-graduate had little hope of church preferment.

The graduate status of an incumbent did not necessarily redound to the advantage of those to whom he preached. The church was still a means of endowing the scholar. Edmund Gunter, Rector of St. George's, Southwark, was a distinguished mathematician who developed the use of sines and tangents and the surveyor's chain, but it was said of a sermon he preached at Oxford University on the Passion that 'our Saviour never suffered so much since his Passion as in that sermon, it was such a lamentable one'. William Oughtred, vicar successively of Guildford St. Mary, Shalford and Albury, was also a mathematician of major talent, the first to use the multiplication and division signs. John Aubrey has given us a lively description of him:

'He was a little man, had black haire, and black eies (with a great deal of spirit). His head was always working. He would drawe lines and diagrams on the Dust. His oldest son Benjamin . . . told me that his father did use to lye a bed till 11 or twelve a clock, with his Doublet on, ever since he can remember. Studyed late at night; went not to bed till eleaven a clock; had his tinder box by him; and on the top of his Bed-staffe, he had his Inke horne fix't. He was more famous abroad for his learning, and more esteemed, than at home. Severall great Mathematicians came over into England on purpose to converse with him. His countrey neighbours (though they understood not his worth) knew that there must be extraordinary worth in him, that he was so visited by Foraigners. When learned Foraigners came and sawe how privately he lived, they did admire and blesse themselves, that a person of so much worth and learning should not be better provided for. He was an Astrologer, and very lucky in giving his Judgements on Nativities; he confessed that he was not satisfied how it came about that one might foretell by the Starres, but so it was that it fell out true as he did often by his experience find; he did beleeve that some genius or spirit did help. The Countrey people did beleeve that he could conjure, and 'tis like enough that he might be well enough contented to have them thinke so. I have heard his neighbour Ministers say that he was a pittiful Preacher; the reason was because he never studyed it, but bent all his thoughts on the Mathematiques; but when he was in danger of being Sequestred for a Royalist, he fell to the study of divinity, and preacht (they sayd) admirably well, even in his old age.'

Some clergy were plainly inadequate. In the parish of Farnham in the 1580s the vicar was 'often overseen with drynke'; at Seale the minister was 'a common gamester and a haunter of alehouses.' John Evans, Rector of Chiddingfold, vanished for a long period to Wales, leaving the parish unserved for three months. He preferred living in an alehouse to his rectory and played with counters for money. In some cases, no doubt, in every period up to the last hundred years, ill-health or mental derangement, too long a period in a parish, perhaps as the only educated person there, or sheer old age - there was no financial provision for retirement and if the clergyman lived to eighty he could still be serving his church - were among the causes of clerical failings.

Many of the clergy were faithful pastors. The Dorking registers pay tribute to Stephen Richman for 'forty yeare painfull travail in his ministry' and John Wilson of Guildford St. Nicholas was described as 'a faithful and a painfull labourer . . . one of a thousand for modesty mildness and meeknes of spirit.' These men were

Puritan in disposition, preferring a simple service and disliking the remains of Catholic practice - the sign of the cross in baptism, the use of the ring in marriage and the wearing of the surplice. John Wilson was suspended from office for a time for refusing to wear the surplice but was restored to his living after receiving a testimonial from Sir George More of Loseley. Robert Horne, Bishop of Winchester from 1561 to 1580, set an example of committed Puritanism. He had spent Mary's reign in exile in the reformed cities of Zurich, Frankfurt and Strasbourg and as bishop ordered the destruction of stained glass in his cathedral and the stone crosses in its churchyard. He disliked vestments although he wore them in obedience to the law. He was one of a group who sought to move the established church in a Puritan direction but remained within the church as loyal members. Other, more radical, spirits were less tolerant of ecclesiastical discipline. John Udall, preacher at Kingston, narrowly escaped execution for felony. After launching violent attacks on his vicar and his archdeacon, he turned his attention, with near-fatal results for himself, on the Queen.

Civil War and Restoration

By the early seventeenth century another form of ecclesiastical rigorist was arising: those clergy, and a few laity, who opposed the Puritans and sought to restore some measure of Catholic doctrine and worship while opposing the claims of the papacy. Lancelot Andrewes, Bishop of Winchester 1619-26, was an attractive example of Anglo-Catholicism, modest and charitable, the leading preacher of his day, the writer of beautiful prayers and widely revered as a saint. Walter Curle, Bishop 1632-47, repaired and decorated his cathedral and removed nuisances and encroachments in the Close. He, with Dean Young, railed in the altar, provided plate, sanctuary hangings and copes, and ordered the prebendaries to make reverence to the altar. In 1636 it was reported by Archbishop Laud, whose name became attached to this movement, that the Diocese of Winchester was all 'peace and order'.

Nicholas Andrews, Vicar of Godalming, is the best-documented of the local Laudian clergy. His Godalming parishioners petitioned the House of Commons against him in 1640, alleging that he had introduced new ceremonies, giving offence by his 'frequent cringeing to the font and communion table', and preaching in a surplice. He denigrated the Puritan taste for sermons, saying that 'he would not leave out the readyng of any one collect for the best sermon that was ever preached'. He was said to be 'popishly affected', having a crucifix hanging in his bedchamber; and was said, somewhat implausibly, to have ridden to Southampton with the parson of Compton to eat fish and make merry, drinking healths to the pope. Perhaps his main offence was his denial of the Calvinism of his opponents, preaching 'false and strange doctrines, saying Fye upon that doctrine that saith that the greatest part of the world shall be damned'. The petition against Andrews is a sign that the 'peace and order' in the diocese was superficial, and during and after the Civil War the Laudian clergy were deprived of their benefices and replaced by Puritans, as Parliament increasingly sought to control the clergy and their teachings. Andrews, who died after lengthy imprisonment, was one incumbent to suffer. Andrews' friend, the Rector of Compton, seems to have been deprived in 1641 and the Vicar of Mickleham in 1642, and Parliament established Puritan lecturers at Farnham and Chertsey. As

Parliament took over control of the county and country in the 1640s more clergy were expelled and replaced by Puritans. In 1646 a Presbyterian system was established, and in 1648 the county was divided into six classes, or administrative areas. Each parish was to have elected elders and ministers.

Both in the 1640s and 1650s attempts were made to reform inequalities in the size of parishes and the wealth of benefices. The large parish of Kingston was to be divided, Little and Great Bookham were to be united,'being situate aboute halfe a mile one from the other and neither of them alone affording a sufficient maytenance for a Godly preaching Minister. . . . And although the parish Church of Little Bookham be but small yet the parish Church of Greate Bookham is large enough to receive the Inhabitants of both parishes. And the way between both the said Churches being good both Summer and Winter'. Effingham and East Horsley were also to be united. The parishioners of Haslemere petitioned Parliament for independence from Chiddingfold: Haslemere was three miles from Chiddingfold 'being very fowle way in the wild [Weald] of Surrey' and was distinct from Chiddingfold 'in all things. . . . save onlie in the parsonage thereof'. Mortlake and Putney were to be divided off from Wimbledon. None of these proposals took effect.

In the 1650s, under the influence of Oliver Cromwell, himself a believer in religious toleration and congregational independence, Presbyterianism, with its belief in an established church and ecclesiastical conformity, was considerably modified by Congregationalism within the parochial structure and, in addition, independent churches proliferated. The Quakers were the most distinctive of the sects which have provided a continuous witness to the present day. George Fox visited Surrey on several occasions and converted a local justice, Thomas Moore of Hartswood near Reigate, in 1655. Other centres of Quakerism in the south of the county included Capel, Dorking, Ockley and Charlwood. A Quaker presence was also maintained in the towns of Kingston, Guildford and Farnham. Quakers were rarely large in numbers but their witness was of a high quality.

At the Restoration of Charles II in 1660 the bishops were restored to their dioceses. Bishop Curle had died in 1647 and Brian Duppa, Bishop of Salisbury, who lived out the preceding years at Richmond, was translated to Winchester. Duppa founded his almshouses at Richmond to commemorate the Restoration. Negotiations took place between the bishops and the Puritans as to the form of worship to be used in the restored church and it was not until two years after the Restoration that a revised Book of Common Prayer was imposed by the Act of Uniformity. Those clergymen who could not accept it were expelled from their benefices on St. Bartholomew's Day (24th. August) 1662 and, together with those who had remained independent of the established church, were subjected to penal restrictions.

Thirty-eight Surrey clergy were ejected. These included the vicars and rectors of most of the town churches, including Dorking, Kingston and Guildford St. Nicholas. A significant minority of the laity were prepared to suffer the civil disadvantages of nonconformity to follow them. By 1676, when the 'Compton Census' was taken by the authorities of the established church, there were about 83,000 'conformists' in Surrey, 4,300 Protestant nonconformists (about 5%) and 130 'Papists' (about 0·2%). In Hampshire, the other half of the diocese, Protestant nonconformists also comprised about 5% of the population but 1% were Papists. The returns may reflect various kinds of bias and must be treated with caution, but the general picture is probably fair enough. The strongest congregations are found where ministers had been ejected from parish churches at the Restoration. At Ewell, where the former rectors of both Ewell and Ashtead were preaching, 48 out of 199 (25%) were dissenters. At Kingston, where the vicar, Richard Mayo, had been ejected, the proportion was nearly 20% (350 out of 1,850) and at Dorking it was 17%(200 out of 1,200).

These congregations suffered a mixture of persecution and grudging toleration during the reigns of Charles II and James II, depending on the political climate. They met largely in private houses, reflecting both their small numbers and the danger of building recognisable chapels. The Corporation Act of 1661 excluded dissenters from public office; the Conventicle Act of 1664 forbade attendance at dissenting worship at which more than five people were present; and the Five Mile Act of 1665 prohibited any illegal preacher from residing within five miles of any city, corporate town or parliamentary borough. Persecution and toleration varied according to government policy but there was significant persecution and, despite periods of 'indulgence' under Charles II and James II, no certainty of tolerance until the Glorious Revolution of 1688.

James II's overt Roman Catholicism was opposed by churchmen and dissenters alike and, following his flight and the accession of William III and Mary, dissenters were rewarded by the Act of Toleration of 1689, which permitted them to establish meeting-houses, provided that they licensed them with the Court of Quarter Sessions or the diocesan bishop. They remained excluded from public office, although many were prepared to meet the requirement of occasional conformity with the established church to overcome this disability.

The Georgian Church

The laity, having seen the results of both Laudianism and Puritanism, and with the example of Roman Catholicism both in their own country's history and contemporaneously across the Channel, were determined that clerical rigorists would no longer dominate them. The Crown, on the advice of the Prime Minister, appointed bishops on the basis of political support and family ties. The eighteenth-century Bishops of Winchester are examples of this policy. Richard Willis was translated from Salisbury to Winchester in 1723 for his role in the passing of the bill of pains and penalties against the Jacobite Bishop Atterbury of Rochester. His successor at Salisbury was Benjamin Hoadly, who had attacked Atterbury in writing. Hoadly, a Whig controversialist whose writings were widely considered to deny any authority to the visible church and even to imply that their author held Unitarian beliefs, succeeded Willis as Bishop of Winchester in 1734. John Thomas (1761-81) had been preceptor to the Prince of Wales and became bishop a year after the Prince succeeded to the throne as George III. Brownlow North (1781-1820) was half-brother of the Prime Minister, Lord North. He had obtained his first diocese in 1771 at the minimum canonical of thirty and, when it was observed that Brownlow was young to be a bishop, his brother replied that when he was older he would not have a brother who was Prime Minister.

The bishops did not neglect their dioceses. The medieval system of visitations and courts continued in force, and a bishop's first visitation of his diocese, his 'primary visitation', was used as an opportunity to obtain basic factual inform-ation about each parish. Bishop Willis, for example, enquired as to the population, the clergy, the provision of schools and charities and the number of dissenters, and his successors issued similar questionaires. The church courts continued to hear cases and to seek to preserve standards of morality. On Sunday 17th. February, 1739, the minister and churchwardens of Ewell certified that Sarah Shepherd, spinster, had stood at the door of the church where most people entered and had stayed there until the first lesson, dressed in a white sheet with a white wand in her hand and 'open-faced', with a paper of accusation on her breast. She had then entered the church and remained throughout the service, standing at the end of the Gospel and confessing the sin of fornication, requesting the prayers of the congregation and leading them in the Lord's Prayer.

Many patrons of rectories and vicarages selected their clergy on the basis of family or other relationship. Barnes was a wealthy rectory in the patronage of the Dean and Chapter of St. Paul's Cathedral: successive eighteenth-century incumbents were appointed from among the prebendaries of the cathedral. Kingston was from 1786 in the patronage of King's College, Cambridge: the college filled the vicarage with five fellows and one other graduate in the course of the following century.

There is no reason to believe that the men appointed were less suitable than those who would have been elected by the parishioners - in some parts of the country clergy were elected popularly and the resulting elections could be almost as corrupt and unedifying as contemporary parliamentary elections. Nevertheless, the priorities expressed in the sales particulars drawn up, like those for any other piece of property, for the sale by auction at a Cornhill coffee shop in 1800 of the right of presentation to Great Bookham were hardly edifying. They describe the value of the tithes, the area of the glebe, the very neat convenient vicarage house and the very excellent garden and orchard, but make no mention of the population of the parish or the commitments of the vicar. Sale particulars for the chapelries of Frensham and Elstead in 1825 stated that the incumbent was aged about sixty, no doubt as an attraction to potential purchasers.

The eighteenth-century clergyman was in many respects still the inheritor of the medieval priest's position in his parish. Like his predecessors he received his income by farming his glebe, or letting it for a rental, and by receiving the tithes of his parishioners. He was presented and instituted to his benefice for life, and usually held it until death. He was responsible for the upkeep of his rectory or vicarage house and the watercolours of the Hassells in the 1820s show that many eighteenth and early-nineteenth-century rectors and vicars had rebuilt, or at least refaced, their houses to resemble gentlemen's houses or large farmhouses in size and appearance. Some clergy neglected their houses. Godstone parsonage in 1795 suffered from the 'very enormous neglect' of the non-resident incumbent. It was dangerous and needed rebuilding at an estimated cost of £900 together with £30 allowed for reusable materials.

The country clergyman's duties might include preparing two long sermons for Sunday but his other religious duties were not necessarily arduous. He might therefore be able to spare the time for secular interests. Gilbert White's *Natural History of Selborne* is a good example from a neighbouring county. In Surrey, John Flamsteed, the first Astronomer Royal, was Rector of Burstow from 1684 until his death in 1719. Owen Manning's *History and Antiquities of the County of Surrey*, completed by William Bray (and now known familiarly as 'Manning and Bray'), is an example of a major work by a Rector of Peper Harow and Vicar of Godalming who 'constantly resided till the time of his death, beloved and

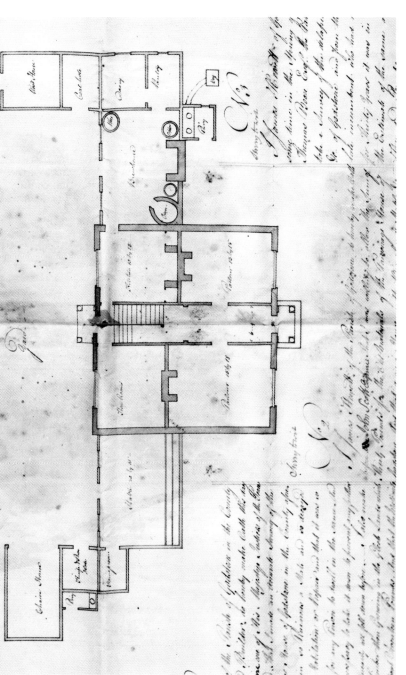

IX GODSTONE RECTORY, 1795: The plan of James Hewett of Godstone, builder and surveyor, for rebuilding the Rectory, which had fallen into a dangerous state of decay during the incumbency of John Kidgell, 'who had not resided nor visited the same for thirty years'. The Rectory is similar to a farmhouse, with a porch and two parlours in front and kitchen and store room behind. One wing contained the stable, harness room, chaise house, knife and shoe hole and a privy. The other wing comprised the brewhouse, with copper, oven and well, pantry, dairy, coal hole and wood house, with a two-seat privy leading to a 'bog'. Hewett's estimate was for £ 900.

X BLECHINGLEY RECTORY, 1821: John Hassell's drawing of the simple Georgian facade.

XI KINGSTON-UPON-THAMES VICARAGE, 1855: The elevation by the London architect, S.S. Teulon, for rebuilding Kingston vicarage. Teulon specified re-use of the existing timber and bricks, which he dated to the reign of Henry VIII, in so far as they were sound, and of three existing bay windows. His estimate, including use of the old materials, was £1250.

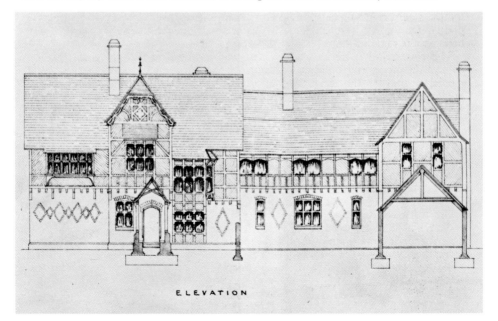

ELEVATION

respected by his Parishioners, and discharging his professional duty in the most punctual and conscientious manner'. Not all clergy fulfilled their duty or employed a curate to do so. William Bannaster, pluralist Vicar of Guildford Holy Trinity and St. Mary and of Wonersh, failed to perform the service at Wonersh on some Sundays. He sometimes preached the sermon on Monday morning 'when great numbers of the poorer sort of Parishioners were getting daily bread by their labour'. Hospitality and charity were expected of the incumbent. It was alleged that Bannaster did not 'keep any hospitality at Wonersh or relieve the Poor or entertain any of his parishioners at Dinner or Supper'.

Church and Society in the Eighteenth Century

The Tudors and Stuarts had made the parish a basic unit of local government. Acts of 1572, 1598 and 1601 placed on parish overseers the responsibility for maintaining the poor and setting them to work. In 1610 they were ordered to keep houses of correction for 'rogues, vagabonds, vagrants and lewd women who have bastards' and in 1662 the parish was made responsible for maintaining all paupers born within its boundaries unless they obtained a legal settlement elsewhere. An Act of 1552 established that parishes were responsible for maintaining their roads and bridges, and in practice the parish was also the unit for policing. An active parish in the eighteenth century, Lingfield, paid a doctor to tend the poor, built a pesthouse, appointed a parish schoolmaster to take school in the vestry room, rewarded those who apprehended felons and organised a fund to hire substitutes for parishioners liable for service in the militia. Their minister did not enjoy the usual sources of benefice income and in 1779 they agreed that he could fence in four acres of land on Lingfield Common 'which should be for the benefit of the Minister residing in the said Parish of Lingfield for the time being'. If the minister were non-resident the land was to be appropriated for the use of the poor. The poverty of the minister therefore gave his parishioners some measure of control over him.

The close relationship between church and society was also expressed in the control the diocesan administration exercised over the professions of teaching and medicine. In 1814 the vicar, churchwardens and overseer, a surgeon and three other parishioners of Walton-on-Thames certified to the archdeacon's court that Joseph Crutchfield was of 'sober honest and virtuous life and Conversation conformable to Doctrine and Discipline of the Church of England as by law established well affected to His Majesty King George III and our present Constitution both in Church and State and as we humbly conceive fitly and duly qualified to teach Latin and English Grammar or other lawful and honest Documents'. Similar licences of 1738 for Charity, wife of Henry Sanders of Shere, as a midwife and of 1778 for John Batchelor of Ockley to practise physic also testify to their orthodoxy and good behaviour as well as to their professional skills.

Parochial libraries were another development of the eighteenth century. The library founded by Andrew Cranston, Vicar of Reigate, in his parish church in the earliest years of the century was a particularly early and notable example. It came to include works of theology and secular erudition and was open both to clergy and laity.

Churches and Worship

From the reformation onwards spending on church building had declined sharply. The aristocracy and gentry, yeomen and merchants rebuilt their houses on a larger scale and in newer styles, but as parishioners they did not for the most part rebuild their churches except when forced to do so by the increase of population or collapse of the fabric. In Surrey, major increases of population were restricted to the metropolitan area, where four churches in Southwark were rebuilt in the eighteenth century and four new churches were built in Lambeth in the early nineteenth century. Other rebuildings were concentrated in the suburban north-east of the county, for example at Kew (1710-14) and Richmond (1750). Elsewhere, Holy Trinity, Guildford, was rebuilt in 1749-63, following a collapse of the tower, Titsey and Long Ditton in the 1770s, Pirbright in 1784 and Egham in 1817-20. Other churches were considerably altered by remedial work. Oxted was heavily restored after a fire in 1719; Kingston was largely rebuilt in the 1720s and Guildford St. Nicholas was greatly altered in 1800. All three were given new towers in the early eighteenth century.

There were fewer church furnishings than in medieval times. At Nutfield in 1712 there was a communion table with a linen cloth to cover it, a cushion and cloth for the pulpit, a surplice, pewter flagon, silver chalice and cover. There were a 'Great Bible', two common prayer books and a book of homilies, and there were five bells. An inventory of Morden Church - a rare example of a church rebuilt in the seventeenth century - in the previous year includes a similar range of goods but adds a bier and black cloth for burials and 'a Pewter Basin for Offertory'. The ringing of bells remained part of village, as well as church, life and in the seventeenth and eighteenth centuries bellfounders such as the Eldridges of Chertsey supplied churches throughout the county. In 1622, for example, Brian Eldridge cast a bell for Lingfield and in 1684 William Eldridge cast a set of six for Woking.

The interior of the Georgian church was filled with high pews. In some churches this took place in a haphazard way as individual parishioners obtained licences, called faculties, from the church courts to erect them. Anthony and Elizabeth Farindon of Batnors in Lingfield were granted a faculty in 1709 to build a pew in consideration of their having presented an altar cloth and communion plate to the parish. At Seale in 1825 E.B. Long filled the north transept with his family pew, 12ft. by 3ft. When a church was systematically repewed at one time, the churchwardens were obliged by law to seat the parishioners according to their social status. At Ash in about 1830 they recorded on a plan of the church that '1s. 3d. poor rate amounts to £145; there are 173 sittings so that each £1 poor rate equals $1\frac{1}{6}$ sitting. If Houses are taken as the Standard of Calculation then Houses 123/Sittings 173 or about $1\frac{1}{2}$ to each House. This seems the most correct view. Providing that persons paying the greatest amount of Church Rate (excepting Persons of Quality) have priority of place during such period of such payments - and such alteration of assessment should ever govern priority of Place'.

The pewing of churches could lead to friction and, after the rebuilding of Dorking parish church in 1837, William Crawford of Pippbrook went to the length of printing a pamphlet to promote his claim to the centre pew in the front of the north gallery, arguing that 'it would be very mistaken delicacy on my part to hesitate' in claiming precedence, and basing his claim on 'the character of my residence, my personal position as a magistrate', and 'the superior accommodation I had in the old church'. Crawford suspected that Arthur Dendy had been given preference because of his larger contributions to the rebuilding fund and he produced complex calculations, based on his existing entitlement to pews, his contribution to the rebuilding fund and the value of pews he had been granted, to support his case.

An impression of a town church in the Georgian period - in the 1820s in fact - can be gleaned from the childhood reminiscences of A.J.B. Beresford Hope of worship in Dorking parish church before the 1837 rebuilding. Hope was not an unprejudiced witness, having reacted against Georgian churches and worship and become an Anglo-Catholic, but his account has a ring of truth. 'The building was a large and had been a handsome Gothic church, but of its interior the general parish saw very little except the nave and aisles, for the chancel was cut off by a perfectly solid partition, covered with the usual sacred writings and some strange painting, among which Moses and Aaron shone in peculiar uncouthness; the eastern portion of the aisles was utilised for certain family pews or private boxes raised aloft and approached by private doors and staircases. These belonged to the magnates of the neighbourhood, who were wont to bow their recognitions across the nave. There was also a decrepit western gallery for the band, and the ground floor was crammed with cranky pews of every shape. The pulpit, of the age of Charles I, stood against a pillar, with the reading desk and clerk's box underneath'.

Sunday worship normally comprised two services, Morning and Evening Prayer. Each might include a lengthy sermon, although in many churches a sermon was preached only in the morning. Morning Prayer would include also the Litany and Ante-Communion. Holy Communion was celebrated at four seasons of the year - Christmas, Easter, Whitsun and Michaelmas - in most villages and monthly in some towns.

The public nature of the Sunday morning service is reflected in Ayliffe's reminiscences of Kingston in 1838. 'At that time it was the custom of the Mayor and Corporation to attend All Saints' parish church every Sunday, and the civic procession was headed from the Town-hall by the parish beadle, George Browne, dressed in a long dark blue coat with gold lace collar and cuffs and a three-cornered cocked hat, and carrying his beadle's staff. Next followed Joseph Walter, the tipstaff, with an ebony staff tipped with silver; then the two mace bearers, Thomas Lock and John Puttock, in long black gowns trimmed with velvet and tall hats with gold bands, and carrying the handsome silver maces. Then followed the Mayor and Corporation, but only the Mayor and Town Clerk were gowned. The procession was met at the church gates by Thomas Beville, the parish clerk, in a black gown trimmed with black velvet and he was attended by Sally Penn, the pew opener, and William Saunders, the sexton. The procession usually started in time to be followed into church by the band and staff of the Militia, and a great number of people assembled in the Marketplace to see it'. According to Merryweather's memories of the same period, farming men came to church in white smocks, embroidered and gathered elaborately by their wives, who accompanied them dressed gaily in red cloaks, straw hats and pattens.

We know little about the music in Surrey churches during the greater part of the Georgian period. The main congregational element in church music was the singing of metrical psalms. The pedestrian sixteenth-century 'Old Version' by

Sternhold and Hopkins was replaced in some churches by the 'New Version' of Nahum Tate and Nicholas Brady. There is little evidence of the activities of church bands and it is only from about the end of the eighteenth century that there is much evidence of organs and choirs. This may be a commentary on the state of research and the survival of the evidence, but it may itself be significant. Richmond installed an organ in 1770 and Kingston acquired its first one since the Reformation period in 1793. In each church the organ was erected in the west gallery and the money raised by voluntary subscription. George III was a subscriber at Richmond. In the early nineteenth century there are signs of greater concern for music. At Wimbledon the salary of the 'Organist and Teacher of the Children' was raised by annual subscription lists, headed by Earl and Countess Spenser. In 1818 Charles Hammond gave £100 to Shere church, the interest to be applied to improving the psalmody. A bass part book dating from 1824 has survived among the Shere parish records and shows that the music consisted of eighteenth-century metrical psalm tunes, some more complex 'fuging' tunes with different parts entering in sequence, and a number of anthems. The Reigate church band was replaced by a barrel organ in 1832 and the singers were given notice and replaced by 'some of the boys and girls from a large and well conducted Charity School in the Parish'. The vicar and churchwardens in their faculty application gave as the reasons the irregularity of the attendance of the singers at Morning Service, their non-attendance in the afternoon and 'the general style of singing, so unsuitable to a spirit of devotion'. Music was generally regarded as an 'optional extra' in worship and outside the scope of the church rate. At Thames Ditton until 1810 the psalms were sung 'without the assistance of any musical Instrument or with the assistance of a Bassoon and a Clarionet by persons not well skilled in the science of music, and not pleasing to the Ears of some of the Congregation'. A barrel organ was purchased by subscription but, 'not being approved of ', was sold in 1812 and a 'finger organ' purchased. The organist, 'a female resident in the Parish', was paid £20 a year from the rate but in 1817 parishioners objected and legal advice was given that it was not advisable to levy a rate for that purpose. At Dorking, Beresford Hope's reminiscences suggest that the church band survived until at least the 1820s: 'A rendering of Tate and Brady (Psalms paraphrased in catchy rhyme and set to weird tunes) was given by an unruly gang of Volunteers with fiddles and wind instruments in the gallery'. The clerk was 'a wizened old fellow in a brown Welsh wig, who repeated the responses in a nasal twang'.

Religious Dissent in the Eighteenth Century

Following the Act of Toleration, 1689, Congregationalists (or Independents), Presbyterians, Baptists and Quakers were no longer prevented from worshipping provided that they registered their meeting houses with either the bishop of the diocese (in Surrey registration was in fact carried out by the archdeaconry court) or the Court of Quarter Sessions. The meeting houses in country areas were for the most part the houses of members of the congregation. As late as 1852 Baptists in Pirbright were worshipping in the 'kitchen or sitting room on the ground floor' of Honers Cottage 'near the Potteries'. Meeting houses were built in towns from the turn of the seventeenth and eighteenth centuries, for example, Congregational ones at Guildford in about 1690 and at Dorking in 1719. The four denominations were all represented in Surrey but none was very strong, except in the metropolitan fringe. In 1725 there were only 40 Presbyterians, 20 Baptists and 15 Quakers in the parish of Guildford St. Mary and Holy Trinity, out of a population of 3,000. Many parishes, such as Pirbright, contained no dissenters.

The Presbyterians, who had been the strongest denomination in the 1660s, declined in numbers and, having lost the position they had briefly enjoyed as the established church, failed to maintain their structure as a denomination and, in some cases, their orthodoxy. Many Presbyterian congregations became Congregational and some became Unitarian: Farnham seems to have been a case in point. The Congregationalists replaced Presbyterians as the main denomination of dissenters in Surrey. They had chapels in most of the towns but less often in the villages.

The Baptists had to live down their origins in antinomian sects who disregarded all secular and religious institutions. In 1708 Farnham and Worplesdon church meeting expelled 'old John Houne' for 'his corrupt principle, namely that a man may take a woman as his wife without any public marriage only private promises one to the other' and for doing so with an unmarried woman. Houne was acting in accordance with an older anabaptist principle which was becoming outdated with the new respectability of the denomination. The same church decided in 1762 that their members were not to be allowed to take part in gaming and plays.

At the end of the century, Dormansland Baptist Church minutes testify to their high standards. In 1797 two members circulated 'unpleasant reports' about a pastor and were adjudged 'blameable in interfering with Brother Chapman's correspondence and marriage in the manner they had done as very serious effects were produced by their continued adherence to dreams, visions and impressions and as they appeared deaf to all admonition on the subject, it was agreed that thay be suspended from the enjoyment of all Church priviledges until they are sensible of the evil of their conduct and renounce their Enthusiastic Oppinions'. 'Messengers' were sent to persuade them to withdraw their allegations but they refused and were eventually 'separated from us'. In 1813 the chapel meeting considered the case of a couple 'who had suffer'd their infant to be Sprinkled in the Church of England - it was generally consider'd as a very inconsistent practice carrying in it a practical denial of their Religious Sentiments as Baptists and tending to give unto the Enemies of Religion sufficient matter for Reproach'. A Sunday School was established there in 1825. A year later it was reported that 195 children had been admitted, of whom 78 could not read at the time of their admission. Ten pupils were given 'Rewards . . . . by which means they have been greatly encouraged, and with which they have purchased the Hymn Books published for Sunday Schools; and your Committee have great pleasure in stating that several of them have repeated the whole of them through, consisting of Two Hundred and Thirty-eight Hymns and others have made great progress therein'. Parish churches such as Mitcham also had Sunday Schools, for secular instruction as much as, or more than, for religious instruction.

The 'three denominations' of Old Dissent had a complex relationship. The word 'denomination' as used in modern times has misleading connotations and implies a degree of organisation absent in the eighteenth century. Congregations were largely independent of each other, although they maintained informal links and the provision of the clergy by denominational colleges, such as Northampton and Hoxton Academies for Congregationalists (Hoxton was later taken over by the Methodists), was one factor making for unity. Congregations could change in doctrine. Presbyterian churches were affected by the rationalist attitude of the period and, as mentioned above, some became Unitarian in belief. Godalming Baptist Church also became Unitarian. Doctrinal changes and personality clashes might lead to divisions or decline. North Surrey dissent was disrupted by William Huntington, an eccentric and predestinarian preacher of great arrogance and dubious morals, who lived for a time at Mortlake, working as a gardener, and who later preached at Kingston, Thames Ditton (where he worked as a coalheaver), Worplesdon, Cobham, Richmond and elsewhere, and whose followers had a seriously disruptive influence at Kingston Congregational Church for several years.

The Quakers stood apart from other denominations. Their refusal to acknowledge the claims of the state in respect of military service and of the church in respect of church rates and taxes led to forcible seizure of their goods. The Guildford Quakers, for example, recorded that in 1705 John Smyth of Godalming had £8 13s. 0d. worth of hay, rye, wheat and barley taken from his meadows and fields by the renters of the tithe. The Quakers, unlike other denominations, had an articulated structure of preparative meetings (usually a single chapel), monthly meetings (covering a number of chapels), quarterly meetings (one or more counties) and national yearly meetings. They cared for their members: James Carpenter, son of an unsuccessful farmer, was apprenticed in 1709 by the Reigate meeting to a Bermondsey shoemaker. They paid his premium and, because he was 'very bare of shirts and other necessaries', the women's meeting provided them for him. The preparative meeting reported to the quarterly meeting on worship, numbers, witness and family life, although by the early nineteenth century the queries put to the Guildford meeting seem to have evoked a fairly standard response quarter by quarter.

The relationship between dissenters and churchmen varied from place to place. Although only the Quakers suffered major penalties for their beliefs, other dissenters continued to be subject to civil disabilities, including exclusion from public office and from universities. In some places there was no doubt a degree of local intolerance amounting to persecution. As late as the 1780s and 1790s the early years of what became the Dormansland Baptist Church show that Baptists could suffer in this way. Elsewhere, better relations prevailed. Practical assistance was extended by the Congregationalists of Chertsey in 1804-6 when Chertsey parish church was demolished and rebuilt, and the congregation of the parish church met in the old chapel on Sunday mornings and afternoons, the dissenters using it in the evenings. Some Anglican clergy, no doubt, were like Gideon Hardinge, Vicar of Kingston, in 'greeting Dissenters not with contumely nor aversion but rather with the greatest friendship'.

Other clergy probably shared the opinion of Thomas Townsend, curate of Pirbright and Worplesdon, who informed his bishop in 1788 that 'a Room is at Rickford Mill, where about eleven years ago, many persons of these and neighbouring parts were accustomed to seek the Lord, as they said, and they were commonly preached to by a Gardener from Kingston [William Huntington]. But I laboured exceedingly to shew the inhabitants the absurdity of deserting their proper Church, without very powerful reasons being offered. The preacher, finding his congregation by degrees with-drawing from him, at length finally withdrew himself from them; and the Room is since converted to the more useful

XII EGHAM CHURCH IN 1828: Edward Hassell's view of the interior of the church, which was rebuilt in 1817-20, shows the shallow chancel, prominent pulpit and reading desk, and the font. There are galleries and box pews. The widening of the central aisle in the foreground may be to allow for benches for the poor.

XIII WESLEYAN CHAPEL, CROYDON, 1831: Interior view looking west, with the pulpit in the foreground and gallery at the west end. The chapel has simple round-headed windows and regular box pews.

XIV ROMAN CATHOLIC CHAPEL, RICHMOND, 1823: St. Elizabeth's, the Vineyard, Richmond, drawn by John Hassell at the time of its construction.

purpose of a Bacon Warehouse and Chandler's shop'. No doubt many Dissenters had an equally unflattering view of the established church. Townsend records of another sect that 'upon being advised to do an act of real christian charity, by presenting to the Bishop of the Diocese every clergyman whom they may find not preaching the Gospel that so the propagation of error may be prevented, they reply, that the "Bishops of the present day are not proper judges, they themselves not being taught of God" '.

By the middle of the eighteenth century the sobriety and conservatism of the establishment and the devout independence of the dissenters were failing to meet the religious needs of the people, although this shortcoming was less noticeable in rural Surrey than in the metropolitan area and in the parishes of the north and midlands which covered wide areas and contained increasingly large populations. What met the need was the tireless energy, preaching genius and organising skill of John Wesley. Wesley, a High-Church Tory by background, rode around England, preaching to Cornish tin-miners, Black-country ironworkers, north-country coalminers and fishermen. He preached in several Surrey towns - the last sermon of his life was preached in Leatherhead - but Surrey was never a strong Methodist county. The structure Wesley built up of circuits, synods and Conference was highly effective for supporting weak and missionary areas; as late as the early 1900s north-west Surrey and north-east Hampshire, a 'wilderness of Methodism', was organised as a missionary area. John Wesley and, more especially, his brother Charles were inspired hymn-writers. Charles Wesley's hymns - records of personal struggle (*Come, O Thou Traveller Unknown*), of the experience of redemption (*And Can It Be That I Should Gain*), and, perhaps most permanently and universally popular, of love (*Love Divine, All Loves Excelling, O Love Divine, How Sweet Thou Art* and *O Thou Who Camest From Above*) - together with the popular tunes to which they were set brought a new emotionalism to worship. The dissenting churches were first to be stirred by this movement of the spirit; the Established Church followed after.

The Methodists revivified local worship even where, as in Surrey, they did not themselves quickly surpass the older dissenting denominations in number of chapels and adherents. In Kingston, for example, the Presbyterian church was in decline by the mid-eighteenth century. William Medcalf was minister from 1760 to 1774 and it was said of him that 'his general strain of preaching was plain and sensible, serious and practical and useful'. The arrival of the Methodists answered, or inspired, a sense of need for more emotional preaching and in 1775 a breakaway group founded a church on Independent, or Congregational, principles, but took as minister a former Methodist preacher.

Eighteenth-century and early-nineteenth-century meeting houses were simple. The interior of Dorking Independent meeting house in the early nineteenth century was surrounded 'except on the side where the pulpit stood' by 'heavy looking galleries painted drab. The pulpit was of the same colour and of a wineglass shape. On either side of it was a large circular hooded window which admitted an abundance of light and gave the place an aspect of cheeriness, which it would not otherwise have possessed. In front of the pulpit was the table pew, where the choir were stationed and whose instruments usually consisted of a clarionet, a bassoon, and if I remember right sometimes also of a flute, and a bass viol; at a later period a clarionet only was used'.

Roman Catholicism continued to be weak in Surrey in the eighteenth and early nineteenth centuries. By the reign of George I there seem to have been nineteen recusant families owning land in the county. Only the Westons of Sutton Place were of any great wealth. Visitations confirm this impression of a few Roman Catholic families but no areas, outside the metropolitan area, of any real strength. Roman Catholic emancipation in 1791 was slowly followed by the setting up of missions and then churches. Refugees from political upheavals across the Channel may have given some encouragement. In 1810 the Bishop of Nantes consecrated the private chapel of his fellow emigré the Prince of Condé at Wimbledon. The chapel, which was on an island in the lake behind Wimbledon House, lasted only four years and fell into disuse when Condé returned to France. Louis Philippe, after being exiled in 1848, resided at Claremont and worshipped at the small chapel founded by James Taylor in 1835 at Weybridge Park, which became associated with the royal family of Orleans.

One small dissenting denomination is particularly linked with Surrey. At a six days' meeting in 1826 for the study of the scriptures at Albury Park, the home of the banker and politician Henry Drummond, Edward Irving, a Presbyterian preacher, Drummond and others in effect originated a grouping which became by 1832 the Catholic Apostolic Church. Irving promoted a prophetic ministry and members of his congregation began 'speaking in unknown tongues'. One of his followers experienced in Rouen Cathedral a revelation that the Roman Catholic vestments worn by the priests were ' the vestments in which the Lord would have his priests serve before him'. Vestments were adopted in Catholic Apostolic churches, notably the church built by Henry Drummond at Albury. A new liturgy was compiled, derived from Roman Catholic and Eastern Orthodox models, and by 1845 the church was observing the Christian seasons and using oil at ordinations and unction and by 1850 using incense and reserving the consecrated elements in a ciborium. In 1851 Drummond published *Principles of Ecclesiastical Buildings and Ornaments*. Like other dissenting churches, Drummond's needed to be registered for public worship, but Drummond treated the requirement in the off-hand manner of a gentleman, rather casually writing, probably to the Clerk of the Peace, to request him to 'be so good as to do what is necessary. . . . to prevent any officious neighbour fining me for the same'.

The Victorian Church

By the end of the eighteenth century the Church of England was itself being affected by a new spirit of Evangelical commitment. The first leaders, merchant families such as the Thorntons, Venns and Wilberforces, lived in Clapham. The Bishop of Winchester from 1827 to 1869, C.R. Sumner, was typical of their energy. While he was bishop, the Diocesan Church Building Society (which also had local committees), the Southwark Fund for Schools and Churches and the Surrey Church Association were all formed to raise funds for church expansion. Church schools were founded in many towns and villages.

Legislative changes permitted over-large parishes to be divided more easily into smaller ones. Previously an Act of Parliament had been needed to unite parishes which were too small, such as Holy Trinity and St. Mary in Guildford, or divide ones which were too large, such as Kingston-upon-Thames. The creation of new ecclesiastical parishes did not now affect the existing local government parochial structure which continued to be based on the 'ancient parish', but the parish was becoming less and less the unit of effective local government. The new Poor Law of 1834 united parishes into Unions for the maintenance of the poor and removed direct responsibility for poor relief from the parish. Parishes were also increasingly united for road maintenance and a county constabulary replaced the parish constable. The endowment of the benefices of the new parishes might be financed by grant from the Ecclesiastical Commissioners, who took over the surplus wealth of the bishoprics and cathedrals, and the building of their churches might be aided by a grant from the Incorporated Church Building Society or a diocesan society. Local subscription would also be needed. The motive for building such churches was often the shortage of church seating: Bishop Sumner declared that 'First among the obstacles which impede the progress of religion in our parishes, I place the want of accommodation in our churches'. In 1837, despite the building of fifteen and the rebuilding of seven churches in Surrey in the previous ten years, there were sittings for fewer than one-third of the population. In the parish of Walton-on-Thames a chapel was built at Hersham in 1838. The reasons given for appealing for funds were 'the great want of sittings in the Parish Church' and that 'the Parish Church being situated on an extreme corner of the Parish, and therefore totally inaccessible to the aged and infirm, affords also to a large portion of the inhabitants of Hersham but a too-ready excuse for absenting themselves from divine worship in their own parish church on the Lord's Day'.

Elsewhere, when an estate was developed for a richer clientele, the developer would supply a new church at his own expense as an attraction to potential house purchasers: a church was one of the facilities potential house-buyers looked for. St. Mark's, Surbiton, was built in 1845 by Coutts and Drummonds, the bankers who were developing the new suburb. Francis Jackson Kent, who developed the private estate of Kent Town, East Molesey, in the early 1850s, built St. Paul's church in a central position there.

The Diocese of Winchester was itself divided and from 1845 to 1877 the increasingly populous metropolitan area, as far as Barnes and Streatham, formed part of the Diocese of London. In 1877, this area, with a large swathe of east Surrey, was transferred to the Diocese of Rochester. This diocese was small in area but very populous, covering the whole of London south of the Thames. In 1905 the Diocese of Southwark was created to cover south London, east Surrey and north-west Kent. New rural deaneries had been already created both in Rochester and Winchester dioceses - the office of rural dean was reintroduced by Bishop Sumner - and regular deanery chapter meetings were held.

In 1851 the National Census was accompanied by a separate census of religious worship. The results were so controversial that the experiment has never been repeated. The form required details of accommodation, free and rented, in each church and, most significantly, the numbers of people attending each service on 30th. March. The results showed that nationally more than half the population did not attend religious worship and that more than half of those who did attended non-Anglican worship. It is not clear which of these results was more shocking to the establishment. In all, the total number of attendances equalled about 60% of the population but, when allowance was made for those who attended more than one service, it was estimated that fewer than half of the population attended a service. Nationally, Church of England attendances amounted to a little below half the total number, Methodists one-quarter, 'Old Dissenters' - mostly Congregationalists and Baptists - one-fifth, and Roman Catholics about 2%. In Surrey the average was lower. Attendances equalled only

54% of the population, lower than in any other county south of the Thames. More than three-quarters of the attendances were Church of England, 15% 'Old Dissent', only 7% Methodist - mostly Wesleyans but including some Primitive Methodists - and 1% Roman Catholic. It was not that the Church of England was particularly strong in Surrey; it was that dissent was far weaker than in any other county. Congregationalists, Baptists and Wesleyan Methodists were, in that order, the strongest of the nonconformist denominations.

Victorian Worship and Belief

The pattern of Anglican worship was changing. The earnest and committed Evangelicals continued as a power in the church, but intellectual and cultural leadership was passing to the children of the Oxford Movement, who valued the Catholic traditions of theology and worship. Several of their leaders, including John Henry, later Cardinal, Newman and Samuel Wilberforce, Bishop of Winchester (1869-73), were children of Evangelical parents who had become aware of deficiencies in their families' tradition. The change in the clergy can be seen at Barnes, where a vibrant hell-fire Evangelical preacher, Henry Melvill, was succeeded in 1870 by a Tractarian Oxford don, Peter Goldsmith Medd, who edited prayers of Lancelot Andrewes and put candles on the altar. In the same year at Guildford St. Nicholas the Evangelical vicar Vincent Ryan was succeeded by the Tractarian J.S.B. Monsell.

The first generation of Anglo-Catholics were concerned to promote 'high' doctrines of the authority of the church and its beliefs and of the objective validity of the sacraments. They were not necessarily concerned with matters of ritual. Their successors translated doctrine into worship. Worship became richer, more orderly and more evocative. Despite the existence of poverty and squalor both housing and clothing were improving for a large proportion of the population and expenditure on church buildings and adornments increased in line with this. Under the influence of the Gothic Revival, medieval churches, from being patched up with Georgian brickwork and round-headed windows, were 'restored' to a 'correct' Gothic form. Many churches were rebuilt, including Dorking and Guildford St. Nicholas, which had already been rebuilt as recently as the 1830s.

Inside, the changes were equally dramatic. J.S.B. Monsell, as Vicar of Egham, commented that his parish church, rebuilt in 1817-20, was 'in no way suggestive of reverence, or helpful to devotion. It cannot but encourage the feeling that God is to be thought of and reasoned about, and understood rather than adored. It seems a place more for instruction than worship; the central spot of which is rather the pulpit than the altar. There is no awe as of The Presence there. The heart does not involuntarily bow, nor the knee bend, under the brooding presence of its solemnity. There are some churches in which a man could not help kneeling; there are others where to sit seems more in keeping with all around. There are some churches in which a man could not look about and whisper to his neighbour, and loll in the corner of his pew, and make himself comfortable; there are others where all of these things seem scarcely out of place. . . . . Work as we may, preach as we may, the very churches in which we lift up our voices are often silently, but sensibly working against us, secularising, rationalising, unsolemnising our people'.

XV THE RECTOR OF EWHURST AND HIS FAMILY: The Rev. J.M. Barlow, Rector of Ewhurst, with his wife and four of their children, Alathea (18), Charles (12), Laura (6) and Harold (14), outside the Rectory in about 1875.

XVI THE LAYING OF THE FOUNDATION STONE OF CHRISTCHURCH, GUILDFORD, 1867.

STOKE D'ABERNON

RESTORATION

OF THE

PARISH CHURCH.

On Sunday, June 28th,

SERMONS

WILL BE PREACHED BY THE

Lord Bishop of Winchester,

AT THE MORNING SERVICE;

AND BY THE

Rev. Morgan Cowie, M.A.

HULSEAN LECTURER,

AT THE AFTERNOON SERVICE;

After which Collections will be made in Aid of the Restoration Fund.

Divine Service in the Morning at Eleven o'Clock, and in the afternoon at half-past Three.

T. HILL, PRINTER, LEATHERHEAD.

THE

First Stone,

OF THE

NEW CHURCH,

OF ST. JOHN,

FARNCOMB

IN THE PARISH OF

GODALMING,

Will be laid, by Divine Permission, at half-past Three o'Clock,

On THURSDAY, MAY 14, 1846.

Prayers will be said at half-past 2 o'Clock, at the Parish Church, after which the Procession will move to the Site of the New Church.

AN ADDRESS

Will be delivered on the Ground, after the usual Prayers,

BY

The REV. JOHN CHANDLER,

VICAR OF WITLEY, AND RURAL DEAN.

STEDMAN, PRINTER.

XVII & XVIII TWO POSTERS: Posters advertising the laying of the foundation stone of St. John's church, Farncombe, in 1846, and the restoration of Stoke d'Abernon Church in 1866.

This was a common feeling of the new generation of clergy. Their answer was to sweep away the high pews and the pulpit, which, with reading desk and clerk's pew below it - the 'three-decker' - had towered over the congregation. The pews were replaced by what we call pews but were then called open benches, all facing the east end. The pulpit was replaced by a lower pulpit on the north side of the chancel arch and a lectern in the form of a brass eagle, imitating medieval examples, on the south side. The galleries, except perhaps for the west gallery, were removed. The chancel was now the centre of attention, with stalls facing inwards as they had in medieval cathedrals and monasteries and housing the choir. At the east end the altar was raised high on steps and enhanced by a reredos.

Some clergy adopted medieval-style vestments and many choirs were robed in surplices. Surrey, outside the area now in Greater London, was not greatly influenced by the extremes of ritualist practice: as late as 1903 vestments were worn in only nine churches and incense was used in none. Guildford St. Nicholas was the only town church in which vestments were worn. Elsewhere, attempts to introduce ritual met strong opposition. In 1901 Admiral L.G. Heath of South Holmwood organised a petition against the vicar's 'hoisting of the ritualist flag' by introducing a cross, candlesticks and flowers on the communion table. Heath was successful in winning his case and in a printed letter 'To the Old-fashioned Protestants' of the parish he congratulated them on the 'hauling down of the ritualistic flag'. Nevertheless many 'Catholic' innovations became widely accepted, the 'cathedral' layout of the chancel and the robed choir in particular. By 1878, A.S.W. Young, Vicar of Kingston All Saints could assure his congregation that 'the time has gone by when it [a robed choir] would have been looked upon as a sign of "ritualist proclivities" '. The moving of the choir to the east end brought it more closely under the control of the clergyman, and the old independent rustic group of singers lost its autonomy but perhaps gained in devotion. Cheap music printing and an army of organist-composers met an ever-increasing demand for service settings, anthems and, for special occasions, oratorios.

Music might be a major attraction in maintaining the congregation of church and chapel and organists were well paid. In 1879, when the organist of St. John the Evangelist, Kingston, was paid £58 6s. 8d. and total expenditure on the choir and organ was £93 12s. 6d., the master and mistress of the boys' and girls' schools and the mistress of the infants' school received among them £260 2s. 11d. and spending on the schools came to £491 0s 4¼d. The comparison may not be completely fair but it is suggestive as to the importance of music in the church.

The most striking development was in hymnody. Hymns were regarded as doubtfully legal in the Church of England until the 1820s although they were already popular with Evangelicals. From the 1820s a large number of hymn books were produced, many of them for individual parishes - in 1839 Lady Katherine Halkett, wife of a churchwarden of Petersham, compiled the *Petersham Hymn Book*. The Tractarians in turn adopted hymnody, in particular translating the ancient hymns of the Western and Eastern churches, and in 1861, *Hymns Ancient and Modern*, the hymn book which would become all-conquering in the Church of England, was published - it was adopted in Petersham in the same year. Two Surrey clergymen were particularly noteworthy hymn writers. At least three hymns of J.S.B. Monsell, Vicar of Egham (1853-70) and Rector of Guildford St. Nicholas (1870-75), have survived into modern hymn books: *Fight the Good Fight, I Hunger and I Thirst,* and *O Worship the Lord in the Beauty of Holiness.* John Ellerton, Rector of Barnes (1876-84), lives on in the evening hymns *O Strength and Stay* (a translation), *Saviour, again to thy Dear Name we Raise,* and, supremely, *The Day Thou Gavest, Lord, is Ended.* Hymn books were indeed the place where different traditions were most effectively united. The eighteenth-century Congregationalist, Isaac Watts, and John Wesley's brother Charles dominated *Hymns Ancient and Modern* as they dominated other books. Conversely, fifteen of Monsell's hymns and fourteen of Ellerton's were included, together with Cardinal Newman's *Praise to the Holiest* and *Lead, Kindly Light,* in the *Congregational Church Hymnal* of 1888.

Patterns of worship changed in other ways. In 1879 the Vicar of Kingston All Saints observed that 'shorter, but more frequent services than of old, seems the wisest and best course for the present day'. Sunday services at his church comprised Holy Communion at 8.30 am., Matins at 11 am., an afternoon service at 3.30 pm. and an evening service at 6.30 pm. The installation of gas lighting permitted the introduction of evening services, intended particularly for the poorer classes. On the first Sunday in the month at Kingston, Matins was followed by Holy Communion and the afternoon service was for children. The beliefs of churchmen had in some respects hardened under the influence of the Evangelical and Anglo-Catholic movements. Eighteenth-century tolerance, even at times scepticism, was replaced by a renewed stress on church tradition by Evangelicals and Anglo-Catholics alike. This renewed dogmatism was confronted by the rise of science. Bishop Wilberforce, while still Bishop of Oxford, had become famous, or notorious, for his attack on the theory of evolution. He was active in condemning an 1860 volume of essays, *Essays and Reviews,* and, a little later, the works of Bishop Colenso of Natal, in which the conclusions of modern geology and Biblical criticism were presented. Nevertheless the contemporary Vicar of Mickleham, while not totally defending Colenso, observed: 'In fact, to compare Colenso's Book with these criticisms on it, the former seeks - in a mistaken way probably - for *truth*; the latter seems rather to consider *effects*!

Evangelical and Anglo-Catholic could unite against scientific threats to belief. They were opposed on other matters. The Evangelical stressed the need for subjective response and personal conversion; the Anglo-Catholic the objective power of the sacraments. The two beliefs conflicted over the doctrine of baptism. In 1848 Bishop Philpotts of Exeter refused to institute to a benefice George Gorham, who denied the objective grace of baptism. His refusal was overturned by the Judicial Committee of the Privy Council, a body in which lay judges were in the majority. This evidence, as many saw it, of lay control over doctrine, enraged and distressed many clergymen. Petition and counter petition circulated among the Surrey clergy. The Vicar of Ash, in refusing to sign the pro-Gorham counter-petition, commented that 'Mr. Gorham appears to me to be simply a *Dissenter*; and the Judgement on his behalf. . . . to *demand* the very strongest remonstrance'. Gorham, incidentally, had been curate at Clapham parish church, the heart of the Evangelical movement, between 1818 and 1827. In the 1860s and 1870s, elections in the Archdeaconry of Surrey to the Lower House of Convocation, the newly revived clerical 'parliament', were seen as straight contests between 'High Church' and 'Low Church'. Although the clergy of the archdeaconry were not ritualists, there seems to have been a small High Church majority. In 1868, Robert Gregory, later to be a noted Dean of St. Pauls, defeated the Evangelical standard bearer, Edward Garbett, Vicar of Christ

Church, Surbiton, and in 1874 J.H. Sapte, Rector of Cranleigh, defeated Garbett by 107 votes to 86.

Church and Society

Charitable work had always centred on the parish church. Benefactors had made bequests to be administered by the incumbent and churchwardens. The Victorian church authorities added to this a more systematic approach to voluntary forms of relief of poverty and encouraged self-help. Maternity clubs provided layettes and nursing care. Penny banks, sickness clubs and coal and clothing savings clubs encouraged thrift and forethought. The position of the church as a centre of social life was enhanced by the provision of lectures and entertainments. Choirs and bell-ringers, long established but traditionally rather independent, were brought more firmly into the ecclesiastical ethos, and in Anglo-Catholic parishes there might also be servers. Guilds and societies were founded for boys, girls, men and mothers. Prayer groups and missionary bodies were set up. Parochial libraries were founded or revitalised. Parish magazines were printed to educate, encourage and entertain parishioners and to keep them informed of church activities. This activity is found in both urban and rural parishes, but it was in towns, with their combination of great needs and great resources, which provided the greatest scope for the organisational powers of the incumbent and his helpers. In Wimbledon, for example, a Maternal Society had been founded in 1821, a Medical Dispensary in 1841 and a Friendly Society in the same year. An Industrial Training School for Girls was established in 1857, the New Wimbledon Needlework Association in 1858 and a Penny Bank in 1859. All of these were described and their accounts were published in the vicar's printed Annual Report in 1861, which also covered the National and Sunday Schools, Clothing, Bedding and Fuel Club, District Visiting Society, Loan Blanket Charity (for the sick and poor in winter), Ladies Working Association, New Wimbledon and Merton Soup Kitchen, Wimbledon Village Club and Lecture Hall, and Wimbledon Cottage Improvement Society Ltd., which bought land in the Ridgeway and built cottages there. The Report of the Vicar of Holy Trinity, South Wimbledon, in 1885, includes similar organisations and also an Employment Registry, Window Garden Society, Temperance Society and Coffee Tavern, Ladies Bible Class, Choral Class and regular social gatherings and entertainments, and vaccination sessions at the Mission Hall. Over all this activity the rector or vicar, secure in his social background and ecclesiastical status, together with those pillars of the community, the churchwardens, ruled, innovated and built.

Yet the incumbent and his wardens were becoming less independent of the body of churchgoers. Church rates, compulsorily levied just as rates were levied for poor relief, highway maintenance and other purposes, had become increasingly a source of conflict, with nonconformists in particular and also with others who opposed the purposes to which the authorities wished to put them. Questions of the propriety of individual items of expenditure being raised by rate were constant sources of friction. At Wimbledon in 1840 it was argued that enlargement of the church should be paid for by voluntary contributions rather than by rate and at Dorking in the 1850s closely fought polls were held to settle the level of church rates; the beadle's and clerk's salaries, the ringer's allowance

29

and the sacramental expenses were voted on. In 1868 the Liberal government abolished compulsory church rates, and the parish churches became more dependent on the willingness of churchgoers, and non-churchgoers of goodwill, to subscribe towards rebuilding, extensions and re-furnishings and other expenses. Financial involvement led to a degree of control, and building and restoration committees were set up, to be followed in some parishes towards the end of the nineteenth century by elected church committees, although these had no legal status. Church control of education was weakened when the same government two years later, by its Elementary Education Act 1870, enacted that elected School Boards were to be founded in parishes which lacked adequate provision of school places. The church school - usually linked to the 'National Society' - continued to be the only one in most villages and in many towns the 'threat' of the school board was averted by heavy programmes of fund raising and school building: this was a major preoccupation of Kingston Church Educational Association.

Nonconformists and Roman Catholics

The Nonconformist denominations shared in the increase in church-building. Eighteenth-century meeting houses in the towns and larger villages were replaced by larger and more imposing churches, especially for Congregationalists and Wesleyan Methodists, and these were supplemented by new churches in the suburbs. These churches were built in the Gothic Revival style, which had been a mark of the Church of England and, to a lesser extent, Roman Catholicism. Many of them, especially the more prosperous town churches, were built with towers and spires and their windows were filled with stained glass. Organs were installed and strong musical traditions developed. Nonconformist churches were also built in villages which had formerly been the preserve of the parish church alone. In the Guildford area, Congregational meetings were held in the 1860s in a barn at Tangley with earth floor, rough seats and a table as a pulpit; 'the familiar sounds of the farmyard adjoining often caused diversion during the services'. At Ryde's Hill, Worplesdon, a wooden chapel costing £160 was used. In the 1870s 'a rustic mission room, formerly an old carpenter's shop', was used and at Merrow, as at Tangley, services were held in a barn. The Methodists also expanded into the villages. Full-time ministers were called in greater numbers and nonconformists took an increasing role in social and political life. They themselves founded schools, such as the Dorking and Godalming 'British' schools. Like the parish church, the chapel was the hub around which a network of social, charitable and devotional activity centred: Tract and Visiting Societies, for visiting homes and leaving tracts; Dorcas Societies, for making articles of clothing for the poor; prayer meetings, missionary meetings, clothing and thrift (or 'slate') clubs, boot clubs and, for young people, Bands of Hope and drum-and-fife bands.

Relationships between Nonconformists and Anglicans were improved by the removal of disabilities on Nonconformists in the course of the nineteenth century and the removal of church rates in 1868 ended another source of conflict. They were able to take an active part in politics and local government - Charles Schofield, a Congregationalist, became in 1836 only the second mayor of Kingston, an office created by the Municipal Corporations Act in the previous year. Nonconformity was in general linked with the Liberal party. Its relative

XIX OBJECTIONS TO RITUALISM - ALTARS IN WIMBLEDON AND ROEHAMPTON: This plate is taken from M.J.F. Mc.Carthy, Church and State in England and Wales, 1829-1906, (London, 1906). The book is an attack on ritualist practices in the Church of England. The author criticised High Church practices in Wimbledon, where he lived.

XX WESLEYAN METHODIST CHURCH, DORKING, 1899: The design of the London architect, Frederick Boreham, for a Wesleyan Methodist church and hall in South Street, Dorking shows a full acceptance of the Gothic style. The church was demolished in the 1970s.

weakness in Surrey was reflected in the weakness of the Liberal party, although nonconformist strength in villages such as Ewhurst was given as one reason for the surprise Liberal victories in the South-West Surrey and South-East Surrey constituencies in the 1906 General Election. Nonconformity had a radical tinge. W.T. Stead, the journalist who exposed child prostitution in London, was the son of a Congregational minister, and during the Boer War he pressed Wimbledon Congregationalists to protest against the War and against conditions in the concentration camps in South Africa. Although some members of the church had reservations about the desirability of putting the matter formally to the church meeting, many of them shared Stead's concern about the camps and the infant mortality in them. The Presbyterians reappeared in Surrey in the later nineteenth century, as Scottish Presbyterians settled in the London suburbs. They remained largely churches for expatriate Scots and their descendants.

Outside the established nonconformist denominations many evangelical meetings existed, especially in towns. They possessed no trained ministry, might have no church or chapel, and often grew and declined with a single leading preacher or small group of enthusiasts. New denominations, more permanent but sharing their evangelical tenets, included the Brethren and, most importantly, the Salvation Army, founded by William Booth. Croydon has a rare example of a 'Christian Mission' chapel founded by Booth before 1878 when he replaced the title 'Christian Mission' with that of 'Salvation Army'.

Roman Catholicism was very weak in Surrey at the beginning of the Victorian period. The County was not greatly affected either by Irish working-class immigration or by the influence of Tractarian converts and by 1851 only 1·4% of church attendances were Roman Catholic. This equalled Hampshire as the highest proportion in any county south of the Thames, but the churches were almost all in the London fringe, in the Richmond and Croydon registration areas, where 7·1% and 4·7% of attendances, respectively, were in Roman Catholic churches. Elsewhere there was a bare couple of hundred worshippers in the whole county on Census Sunday in 1851. There was increased growth in the second half of the century and by the turn of the century impressive churches, such as Sacred Heart, Wimbledon and St. Joseph's, Dorking, witnessed to the increased numbers, wealth and self-confidence of Roman Catholics. Anti-Catholic feeling still surfaced from time to time - in South Wimbledon in the early 1900s a proposal to make a grant to a school in Russell Road aroused attacks on 'Rome on the rates' - but well-loved parish priests such as Fr. Kerr at Wimbledon and Fr. Volckeryck at Dorking won the respect and love of their townsfolk of all denominations.

Epilogue

By the end of the nineteenth century the churches, although perhaps they had barely kept pace with the growth of population, were strongly entrenched in all levels of respectable society. Yet only about 10% of the national population made their Easter Communion as Anglicans. Nonconformist membership was about 6-7%, although Sunday by Sunday nonconformists probably equalled or surpassed Anglican attendance figures. Roman Catholics, concentrated in areas of traditional recusancy and Irish immigration, may have equalled these. Perhaps one-quarter of the population, therefore, showed a degree of commitment to the churches. The fast running of the previous half-century had left the churches less strong proportionally than they had been in 1851. In Surrey the Anglican proportion would have been higher and the Roman Catholic one much lower.

Between 1919 and 1921 the Church of England adopted a more democratic structure. An elected General Assembly was given legislative and governmental powers and parochial church councils were elected to take over most of the duties of churchwardens in parishes. Two intermediate tiers, Diocesan and Ruri-decanal Conferences, were also established. The most visible organisational change of the twentieth century in Surrey was the further dismemberment of the Diocese of Winchester in 1927, when the Surrey portions of the diocese, together with a number of parishes in north-east Hampshire, formed the new Diocese of Guildford.

The last twenty years have perhaps seen the greatest rate of change since the end of the nineteenth century in both the language and ethos of worship. There has been a further sharp decline in church attendances, although Surrey and outer London have seen less decline than the metropolitan area. In inter-church relations there have been one inter-denominational merger, of Congregationalists and Presbyterians into the United Reformed Church, a number of local mergers, such as Egham United Church (Congregational and Methodist), and a general development of co-operative activity. The churches are, as in all previous ages, in part influencing and in part reflecting their environment, but the story of the churches in the twentieth century at local level needs further research and only when many more local histories have been completed will synthesis, or even the brief sketch attempted for earlier periods in this booklet, be possible.

XXI SHAMLEY GREEN CONGREGATIONAL MEETING, 1891. A Congregational chapel was erected in 1836, adjoining a farmyard. After a decline in Congregational strength locally, the building was used in the 1850s and 1860s by the Strict Baptists and for a time was used by both denominations at different times of the day. The Congregationalists regained title to the building and Revd. Henry Bell, evangelist under the Guildford minister, is said to have gathered a congregation of some 300 people and preached to one half of his congregation inside the building and the other half outside.

NOTES

THE BEST GENERAL HISTORY of Christianity in England is D.L. Edwards, *Christian England*, 3 vols. (London,1981-4, paperback 1982-5). This covers the period to 1920. (The author is Provost of Southwark Cathedral). For the period since the First World War, the standard work is Adrian Hastings, *A History of English Christianity,1920-1985*, (London,1986, paperback 1987). For Surrey, the only general work is *The Victoria County History of Surrey (V.C.H.)* vol. II. (London,1902), p.1-130. This also includes accounts of the religious houses of the county, which I have not covered. There are many articles on the history and antiquities of Surrey churches in *Surrey Archaeological Collections (S.A.C.)* published by the Surrey Archaeological Society. Most of the Bishops of Winchester are included in the *Dictionary of National Biography (D.N.B.)*, (Oxford, 1885-1901) with supplements. Although out-dated this is a useful starting-point.

The main locations of original source material are: Surrey Record Office, at County Hall, Kingston-upon-Thames, and Guildford Muniment Room, Castle Arch, Guildford; Greater London Record Office, 40 Northampton Road, London, EC1; and Hampshire Record Office, 20 Southgate St., Winchester. Parish records are deposited in the Surrey Record Office: records of parishes in the Diocese of Southwark (outside Inner London) and of parishes in the rural deaneries of Emly and Epsom in the Diocese of Guildford are deposited at County Hall, Kingston-upon-Thames; records of parishes in the Diocese of Guildford (other than the rural deaneries of Emly and Epsom) are deposited at the Guildford Muniment Room. Records of those Inner London parishes which were formerly in Surrey are in the Greater London Record Office. Records of the Archdeaconry of Surrey and probate records of the Archdeaconry Court and the Commissary Court of the Bishops of Winchester in Surrey are held at the Greater London Record Office, and are an important source from the sixteenth century onwards. Records of the Diocese of Winchester are held at the Hampshire Record Office: the medieval bishops' registers are an important source and there is some useful material, notably visitation returns, for the post-Reformation period. Records of Nonconformist churches, when they are deposited in a record office, are mostly in Surrey Record Office at County Hall, Kingston-upon-Thames (for East Surrey) and Guildford Muniment Room (for West Surrey).

p 1-4	Much of this section is based on the research and doctoral thesis of W.J. Blair, *Landholding, Church and Settlement in Surrey before 1300.* Oxford Ph.D. (1982). Dr. Blair's work is to be published by the Surrey Archaeological Society in the near future.
p 5, line 39-42	See R.J. Milward. *Early Wimbledon.* (Wimbledon. 1969).
p 6, line 7-20	*Surrey Archaeological Collections (S.A.C.).*XXV. 3-32.
p 6, line 20-40	F.M. Powicke & C.R. Cheney, *Councils & Synods*, (Oxford, 1964), Vol. I. 127-8, 407, 721.
p 7	For architectural details see I. Nairn & N. Pevsner, *Buildings of England: Surrey,* (Harmondsworth, 1969).
p 7, line 16-20	For the most detailed recent interpretation, which regards the theme as a ladder of salvation, see *S.A.C.*, LXXII. 127-156.
p 7, line 32-35	Kingston Borough Archives KG 2/1.
p 7-8	The inventories drawn up in the reign of Edward VI are the main source for ornaments and vestments at the close of the middle ages. See *S.A.C.* IV. 1-189; XXI. 32-82; XXII. 69-104; XXIII. 30-60; XXIV. 1-39.
p 8, line 12-16	Guildford Muniment Room (GMR) 1225/1/2a,b.
p 8, line 30-36	*Councils & Synods*, I, 136, 722.

p 8-9	Greater London Record Office (GLRO). Archdeaconry Act Book, 1511-1515.
p 9	J.A.F. Thompson, *The Later Lollards, 1414-1520*, (Oxford, 1965). Hampshire Record Office (HRO), Reg. Foxe, fo. 69.
p 10-13	Much of the information regarding the clergy is taken from the thesis of R. Christophers, *Social and Educational Background of the Surrey Clergy, 1520-1620*, London Ph. D. (1975). The information on wills and on the condition of church buildings comes also from this thesis. There is a copy in the library of the Surrey Archaeological Society, Castle Arch, Guildford.
p 10-11	*S.A.C.*, XXII, 74.
p 11, line 7-10	R.J. Milward, *Tudor Wimbledon*, (Wimbledon, 1972).
p 11, line 12-18	Royal Borough of Kingston-upon-Thames Archives: Churchwardens Accounts, KG 2/2/2-3.
p 11, line 30-34	*V.C.H.* II. 20.
p 12	For Oughtred and Gunter, see Aubrey, *Brief Lives*. (ed. O. Lawson-Dick), (London, 1949, paperback 1962).
p 13, line 28-29	GMR Loseley Manuscripts, LM 590.
p 13-14	*S.A.C.* XVII, 102-6.
p 14	See B. Williams, *Quakers in Reigate, 1655-1955*, (Redhill, 1980).
p 14	The Compton Census has been edited: A. Whiteman (ed), *Compton Census of 1676*, (Oxford, 1986). For Congregationalism in Surrey, see E.E. Cleal, *The Story of Congregationalism in Surrey*, (London, 1908).
p 15-16	HRO, B/2/A-2, for the returns to Willis' questionnaire.
p 16, line 3-10	GLRO, DW/OP/1739/4.
p 16, line 12-14	For the clergy of Barnes, see J. Whale, *One Church, One Lord*, (London, 1979).
p 16, line 20-28	GMR, PSH/BK.G/10/5; Surrey Archaeological Society, Parish Boxes.
p 16, line 31-35	For the Hassells, see *A Catalogue of Pictures of Surrey and elsewhere by John Hassell (1767-1825) and his son Edward (1811-1852)* in *S.A.C.* LXXV, 3-55.
p 16, line 35-8	GLRO, DW/OP/1795/3.
p 17, line 2-9	GLRO, DW/OP/1741/1 and 1743/1.
p 17, line 19-28	SRO, Lingfield vestry book, 2399/7/1.
p 17, line 31-41	GLRO, DW/OP/1814/13;1738/25;1778/15.
p 18, line 1-16	A readily available and comprehensive set of illustrations of Surrey parish church exteriors at the end of the Georgian era is available in C.T. Cracklow, *Views of Surrey Churches*, ed. K. Gravett, (Chichester, 1972).
p 18, line 17-21	SRO, Nutfield inventory of church goods, P26/6/1.
p 18, line 21-24	SRO, Morden inventory of church goods, 2269/10/3.
p 18, line 24-27	SRO, Lingfield parish, Bond, 2399/6/1; Woking churchwardens' accounts P52/7.
p 18, line 30-33	GLRO, DW/OP/1822/9.
p 18, line 33-34	GLRO, DW/OP/1825/7.
p 18, line 36-43	GMR, Ash parish records, plans of seating, PSH/MS/15/6,7.
p 19, line 18-19	GMR, Dorking parish records, restoration papers, PSH/DO.M/12.
p 19, line 8-23	Quoted in N.G.J. Stiff, *The Church in Dorking and District*, (London, 1912),44-6.
p 19, line 30-44	G.W. Ayliffe, *Old Kingston*, (Kingston-upon-Thames, 1914),21.
p 19, line 45-47	F.S. Merryweather, *Half a Century of Kingston History*, (Kingston, 1887).
p 19	For music in parish churches in general, see N. Temperley, *The Music of the English Parish Church*, (Cambridge, 1979).
p 20, line 6	For Richmond, see A.C. Piper, *History of Richmond Parish Church*, (Richmond, 1887).
p 20, line 6-7	For Kingston, SRO, Vestry book, P33/4/1.
p 20, line 10-12	SRO, Wimbledon church officers' papers, P5/5/641-663.
p 20, line 12-16	GMR, Shere parish records PSH/SHER/53/1.
p 20, line 16-22	GLRO, DW/OP/1832/7.
p 20, line 22-29	SRO, Thames Ditton parish records 2568/4/3.
p 20, line 29-34	Stiff, *op.cit.*,45.

p 20-24	For Protestant dissent, from the Reformation to the end of the eighteenth century, see M, Watts, *The Dissenters*, (Oxford, 1978), and for Roman Catholicism over a slightly longer period, see J. Bossy, *The English Catholic Community, 1570-1850*, (London, 1979).
p 20, line 41-43	GLRO, DW/OP/1852/15.
p 21, line 2-4	HRO, B2/A-2..
p 21, line 13-20	GMR, Minute book of Meadrow Unitarian (formerly Baptist) Church, Godalming, 143/1/1.
p 21, line 21-41	SRO, Minute book of Dormansland Baptist Church, 2615/1.
p 21, line 42-43	SRO, Mitcham Sunday School minute books,1788-1871, P46/8/1-4.
p 22, line 6-12	*D.N.B.*sn, William Huntington.
p 22, line 13-28	GMR, Monthly minute books 124/1/1; 124/2/1. B. Williams, *op.cit.*
p 22, line 35-39	*The Book of Chertsey*, (Chertsey, 1929),56.
p 22-3	HRO, B1/A-2.
p 23, line 32-38	A.C. Sturney, *270 Years. The Story of Kingston Congregational Church*, (Kingston-upon-Thames, 1932),19.
p 23, line 40-48	T.R. Grantham, *Dorking Congregationalism*, (Dorking, 1913),21.
p 23-4	*V.C.H.*,II,43; R.J. Milward, *Portrait of a Parish, Jesuits in Wimbledon, 1877-1977*, (Wimbledon,1977),8-9.
p 24, line 13-31	For Catholic Apostolic furnishings and Drummond's *Principles*, see P.F. Anson, *Fashions in Church Furnishings, 1840-1940*, (London, 1960), 107-114. The book is an excellent guide to the relationship of styles of church furnishing, mostly Anglican and Roman Catholic, and contemporary fashion. Anson (p.132) suggests that the size of the crinoline was probably the main reason for open benches replacing box pews in new churches in the 1860s (c.f. below p27, lines 1-3). For Drummond's letter see SRO, AS6/13/24.
p 24, line 9-19	SRO, Hersham parish records, 2843/4/2,5.
p 25-6	Public Record Office, HO129. For an analysis, see B.J. Coleman, *Southern England in the Census of Religious Worship, 1851*,in *Southern History*, V, (1983).
p 26, line 33-47	F. Turner, *Egham, Surrey*, (Egham, 1926), 172.
p 27, line 13-16	W.N. Yates, *Bells and Smells*, in *Southern History*, V, (1983).
p 27, line 17-22	GMR, Holmwood parish records, PSH/HO/7/3.
p 27, line 24-26	All Saints', Kingston-upon-Thames parish magazine, 1878.
p 27, line 37-38	SRO, 2806/5/2. St. John's, Kingston-upon-Thames parish magazine, 1874.
p 27, line 42-44	C.D. Warren, *History of St. Peter's Church, Petersham, Surrey*, (London, 1938), 79.
p 28, line 10-17	All Saints', Kingston-upon-Thames parish magazine, 1879.
p 28, line 26-29	GMR, Mickleham parish records, PSH/MIC/38/13.
p 28, line 38-42	GMR, Ash parish records, PSH/AS/23/9-11.
p 28-9	*Surrey Comet,* 28th, February 1874.
p 29, line 20-35	SRO, Wimbledon parish annual reports, 2067/5/6,8.
p 29, line 44-46	SRO, Wimbledon parish records, P5/2/161;P5/15/66.
p 29-30	GMR, Dorking parish records, poll books, PSH/DOM/8/11-16.
p 30, line 14-15	SRO, Kingston Church Educational Association minute book, 3047.
p 30, line 27-32	E.E. Cleal, *op. cit.*,395,397,399.
p 31, line 1-3	H. Pelling, *Social Geography of British Elections, 1885-1910*, (London, 1967).
p 31, line 4-10	SRO, Minute book of Worple Road Congregational Church, Wimbledon, deacons' meetings, 2151/4.
p 31, line 19-21	A. Davies, *The Story of the Churches in Croydon*, (Croydon, 1985), 15.
p 31, line 31-38	R.F. Philpott, *St. Joseph's, Dorking, A Cemtenary History of the Church and Parish, 1872-1972*, (Dorking, 1972); R.J. Milward, *Portrait of a Parish, Jesuits in Wimbledon, 1877-1977*, (Wimbledon, 1977).

INDEX

of Places in Surrey